ColourSpectrums ™

Book 1: The Introduction

Rob Chubb

Also in the ColourSpectrums series:

*ColourSpectrums Personality Styles Book 2:
Stress Management and Conflict Resolution*

*ColourSpectrums Personality Styles Book 3:
Brightening Pale Colours*

 FriesenPress

Suite 300 - 990 Fort St
Victoria, BC, Canada, V8V 3K2
www.friesenpress.com

Copyright © 2016 by Rob Chubb
First Edition — 2016

All rights reserved.

No part of this publication may be reproduced in any form, or by any means, electronic or mechanical, including photocopying, recording, or any information browsing, storage, or retrieval system, without permission in writing from the publisher.

ISBN
978-1-4602-4986-4 (Hardcover)
978-1-4602-4987-1 (Softcover)
978-1-4602-4988-8 (eBook)

Distributed to the trade by The Ingram Book Company

To Mr. O and Mr. A

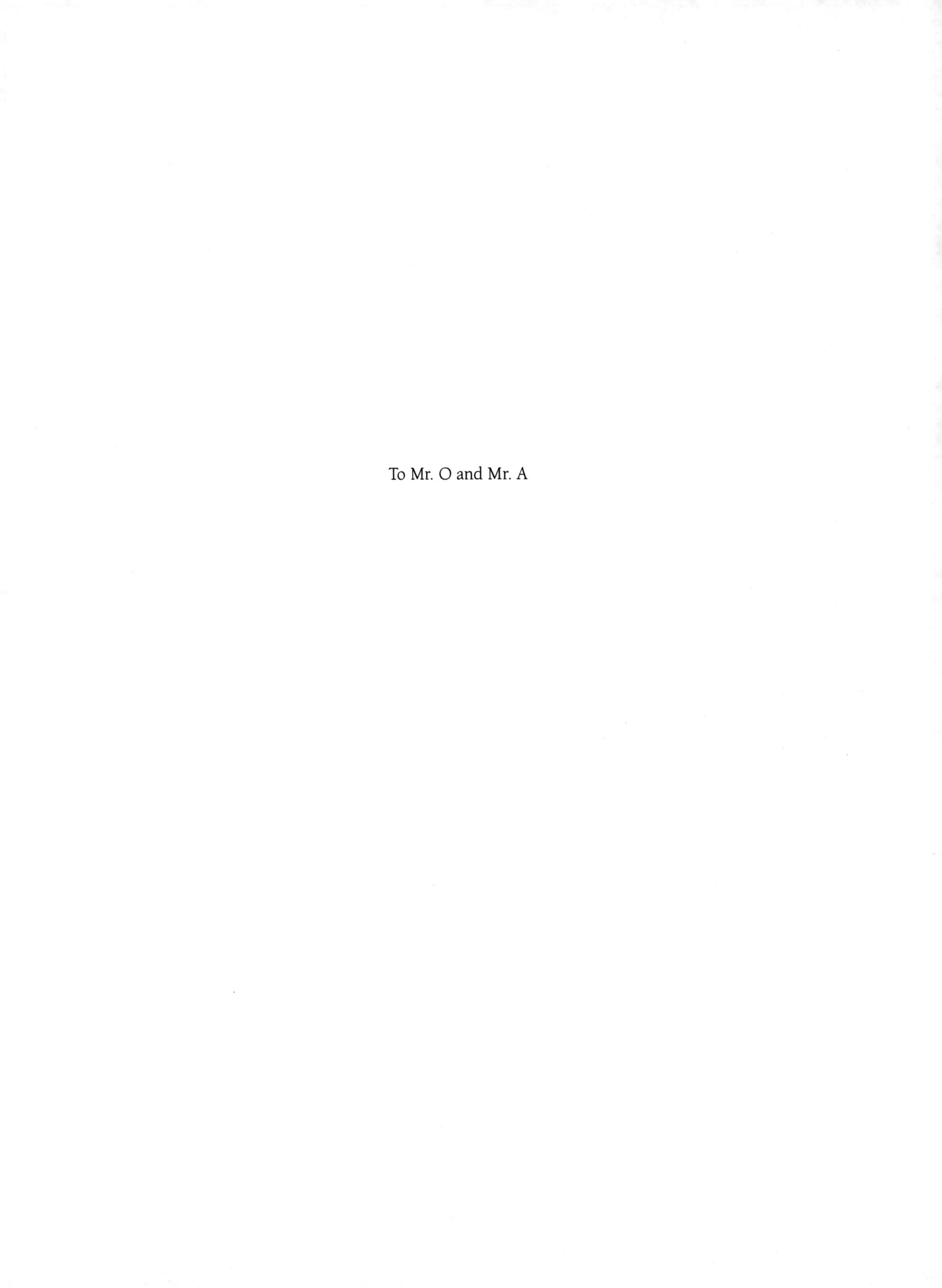

Contents

> *I am not a Jungian... I do not want anybody to be a Jungian. I want people above all to be themselves.*
>
> — Carl Jung

Acknowledgements . . . . *i*

How to Get the Most Out of This Book . . . . *iii*

Introduction: What Is ColourSpectrums? 1
    The ColourSpectrums Symbol 2
    The Philosophy of ColourSpectrums 3
    ColourSpectrums: A Metaphor That Enhances Learning 5
    The History of ColourSpectrums 7
    The History of Quadra Models 10
    Quadra Models: One Common Theme, Two Different Philosophies 10
    The History of Colours 12

Section 1: Revealing Your ColourSpectrums Personality 15

The ColourSpectrums scoring system is a process of self-discovery.

    Attribute Card Illustrations 15
    Completing the ColourSpectrums Scoring System 29
    The ColourSpectrums Scoring System: How and Why It Works 33
    Circle Blend 38
    ColourSpectrums Day-to-Day 43
    Displaying Your ColourSpectrums Personality 44

Section 2: ColourSpectrums Implications for You and Others 47

ColourSpectrums: Complex But Not Complicated

- How Many ColourSpectrums Are There? 47
- Brightest Colour Presentations 52
- Using the ColourSpectrums Language 63
- Card Descriptions In Detail 64
- Five Distinct and Separate Senses 66
- Four Distinct and Separate Colours 67
- Four Distinct and Separate Developmental Functions 69
- Proverbs 71
- Endings and Beginnings 74
- ColourSpectrums Applications 74
- ColourSpectrums Attribute Card Set 81

Acknowledgements

I first started delivering ColourSpectrums workshops in 1990, first to my colleagues at what was then Grant MacEwan Community College. Over the years the approach changed somewhat, but the core idea of ColourSpectrums remained the same.

This series of books would not have been possible without all those people who have been part of ColourSpectrums along the way.

All my workshop participants — from the early MacEwan days and beyond — have made this book better by sharing their enthusiasm and feedback. Some of these people have shared their experiences, which are included in the book and make it more meaningful and relevant. My workshop facilitators have helped me deliver ColourSpectrums to more and more people, and their insights have improved my delivery materials.

My wife of 34 years, Laurie, has been unfailingly supportive as this venture took up more and more of my time and even as ColourSpectrums changed from a diversion to a career. Thank you, Laurie, for the colour you bring to my life and for our five wonderful children.

And speaking of those wonderful children — since I started working on these books, they've grown and the family has expanded to include grandchildren. Yes, it's taken longer than I would have expected to turn my notes into a bound book. Without the gentle nudging of my editor I might still be making "just one more change... ." Thank you, Shelagh, for your direction, commitment and undying faith in this project.

Rob Chubb

How to Get the Most Out of This Book

Card Sets

In this book, I refer to the cards participants use in my workshops. A set of four two-sided attribute cards is provided on the last eight pages of this book. Print-on-demand books display these cards on the back cover as well. For a more hands-on ColourSpectrums experience, purchase coloured card sets at www.colourspectrums.com

Quick Start Instructions

The introduction describes the philosophical and historical underpinnings that set the stage for subsequent sections. If you just can't wait to reveal your ColourSpectrums personality, jump ahead and begin at Section One to complete the ColourSpectrums scoring system. You can return to the introductory information later. On the other hand, if you can suspend your curiosity for a few pages, then read the introduction to establish a deeper initial understanding first. Above all, enjoy the learning and make this book work for you.

This symbol indicates a written exercise. Complete written exercises to maximize your understanding and integrate your skills.

This symbol indicates a solitary exercise. Complete solitary exercises to integrate information and personalize your learning.

This symbol indicates a paired exercise in which you talk or interact with a partner. I encourage you to complete these paired exercises with someone important to you — your spouse, your best friend, your child, your brother or sister, your mom or dad, or a colleague. Sharing these experiences with someone will maximize your learning while enhancing your personal/professional relationship. For exercises that require a worksheet from the book, make a copy so you each have one.

Introduction: What Is ColourSpectrums?

ColourSpectrums is a personality styles and human development model presented to groups in an entertaining and interactive workshop format. ColourSpectrums is a dynamic model for personal growth and professional development. Carl Jung's primary psychological colours are used as a metaphor to represent the four classic dimensions of personality development:

Blue Emotional Development
Green Intellectual Development
Red   Physical Development
Yellow Organizational Development

In a ColourSpectrums workshop, participants interact in a guided process of self-reflections, group discussions and activities that celebrate diverse personality strengths and create solutions to human challenges. Each participant sorts the four colourfully illustrated attribute cards to reveal their ColourSpectrums personality. Each colour spectrum is a particular blend of these four colours that is unique to each individual.

ColourSpectrums is an enchanting colourful language for enhancing communication and interpersonal effectiveness. Children, youth and adults alike have been using ColourSpectrums for years to effectively expand personal understanding and enhance interpersonal communication skills.

This book will guide you through the same exciting process of positive self-discovery that has been experienced by thousands of workshop participants. You will discover your natural personality strengths and challenges. You will understand the unique colour spectrums of other people, their natural strengths and challenges. Regardless of your age, profession, lifestyle, strengths and challenges, you will benefit from this ColourSpectrums experience.

This process will make you more effective, personally and professionally. You will be able to use ColourSpectrums immediately to improve your quality of life at home, at school, at work and in the community.

The ColourSpectrums Symbol

The ColourSpectrums Symbol represents the importance of diverse personality attributes in two areas: personal diversity and team diversity.

Personal Diversity

Check the colour representation of the ColourSpectrums symbol — you will find this on this book's cover. The four psychological primary colours of the human figure represent the four attributes essential to human growth and personal effectiveness. The blue arm reaches out to embrace relationships. The red arm stretches upward, seeking action. The green analytical attribute grounds us in reality. The yellow leg is tradition, on which we firmly stand.

Team Diversity

The unique blending of colours within each letter depicts the unique blend of personality attributes that each of us has. Just as each letter is unique and essential to the creation of the word "ColourSpectrums," we are each unique and essential to the creation of effective relationships and teamwork.

The whole is greater than the sum of the parts.

ColourSpectrums and colour spectrums

Throughout this book, we write ColourSpectrums to refer to the personality styles and human development model and colour spectrums to refer to each person's spectrum of colours. You have your own colour spectrum, and you understand it through studying ColourSpectrums.

The Philosophy of ColourSpectrums

ColourSpectrums is based on four fundamental principles.

1. Nature, nurture and "free will" influence personality development.

There is no one like you; there never has been, and there never will be. The reason is that your personality has developed, and continues to grow and develop, through a dynamic combination of three major areas of influence: **nature, nurture,** and **free will**.

Your personality is shaped, in part, by nature. You have genetic characteristics you inherited from your biological parents and their ancestors. The most obvious genetic characteristics are your physical features. Some physical characteristics remain constant throughout your life: your gender, your race, your blood type and your fingerprints for example. Other physical features change throughout your life in genetically programmed ways: your weight, your height, your body proportions, your skin texture, your hair colour and so on.

The less obvious genetic characteristics are your personality characteristics. Genetics influence your emotional development, intellectual development, physical development and organizational development and functioning. Some personality characteristics remain relatively stable, some change over time and some change from moment to moment. ColourSpectrums acknowledges and incorporates these influences of nature on your personality.

Your personality is also shaped, in part, by nurture. Nurture consists of your life experiences in your family of origin, your community and your culture. These environmental influences begin at conception and continue throughout fetal development, infancy, childhood, young adulthood, adulthood and old age, continuously shaping your personality development throughout your entire life. Nurture, in this context, includes both positive and negative influences, both nurture and lack of nurture. ColourSpectrums incorporates these influences of nurture.

Nature and nurture always make the textbooks. Attempts to explain human behaviour are often put to the test question, "Is behaviour the result of nature or nurture?" It is generally agreed that human development and behaviour is influenced by the combined influences of both nature and nurture. ColourSpectrums recognizes and incorporates the influences of both.

Consider, however, that nature and nurture are both external forces — nature refers to the genetic cards you were dealt and nurture is what happens to you. It is also important, therefore, to consider the effect of free will. We are not simply passive beings adrift and tossed about in the sea of life at the complete mercy of the external forces of nature and nurture. The view that we are simply the result of these external forces denies our human spirit and our ability to make choices. As human beings, of course, we make individual choices that emanate from deep within, that originate from our internal forces of intention and spirit.

Free will is our power of intention to influence from within. Your will and intentions actively influence your personality development. Your choices — what you choose to do — have profound implications because your choices result in life experiences that further influence your personality. You have "free will" — the power and freedom to will yourself to do things, the power to manifest what you will. You can do what you will. Because you have free will you also have "free won't" — the power and freedom to choose what you will not do, the power to manifest what you will not. Your willpower and "won't power" empower you to choose. You are willing yourself to read this book. Your free willingness to read this book will make a difference and will influence your personal growth. ColourSpectrums values and incorporates the influences of free will.

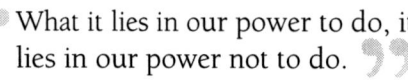

> What it lies in our power to do, it lies in our power not to do.
>
> — Aristotle

2. You have a unique personality.

Take pause to consider the combined influences of your own nature, nurture and free will. Of the billions of people on the planet Earth, no one has ever had, or ever will have, the same genetic characteristics, the same nature as you. No one has ever had, or ever will have, the same nurturing experiences that you have had, are having and will continue to have. And, even if we cloned everyone, no one would ever make the same free will choices that you are making throughout your life. So of the billions and billions of people in the world, there is no one like you, there never has been, and there never will be. In a universe of infinite diversity and endless possibilities, you are now and forever unique for eternity. This is a heavy burden or a wonderful opportunity depending on your attitude. ColourSpectrums values the uniqueness of each and every individual human being.

> Every individual human being born on this earth has the capacity to become a unique and special person, unlike any who has ever existed before or will exist again.
>
> — Elisabeth Kübler-Ross

3. You strive to achieve self-fulfillment from your unique perspective.

ColourSpectrums supports the belief that each person strives to achieve a positive sense of self-worth and self-esteem from his or her unique perspective. You are striving to be the best person you can be. Because each person has a unique combination of nature, nurture and free will, we each strive to achieve our potential, self-fulfillment and meaning in life in unique and diverse ways, in as many different ways as there are people.

4. You are the expert regarding your own experience.

You know yourself better than anyone because you spend more time with yourself than anyone else. Different people will know you at different ages and stages of your human development — as a child, a young person, an adult, or as an elderly person. Throughout your life you accumulate a vast wealth of life experiences that are integral to who you are and who you are becoming. You are the only person who has the benefit of knowing these rich diverse experiences. You know the inside story and have the big picture.

Some people know what you are like at home, some people know what you are like at work or at school, and some people know what you are like at a party on Saturday night. You are the only person who knows what you are like in all situations: all of your emotions, all of your thoughts, all of your behaviours and all of your plans. The rest of us can observe you, make best guesses, provide feedback and experience similar events, but only from our own unique perspectives. You are the expert regarding your own experiences and you know yourself best.

ColourSpectrums: A Metaphor That Enhances Learning

ColourSpectrums facilitates learning that is rapid, easy and accessible, meaningful, painless, fun, and long-lasting.

Rapid: The use of colours as a metaphor for understanding complex human behaviours and dynamics facilitates learning. Colours are rapidly and uniquely processed in the brain.

Easy and Accessible: ColourSpectrums is easy to use. It is used by children as young as four years of age, persons with learning disabilities, persons with mental disabilities, people with diverse religious, ethnic and cultural origins, people who are illiterate, people who are well educated, and people who are highly effective in business, education, human services and government. Everyone can learn the enchanting language of ColourSpectrums because it taps into a universal language that everyone can identify with...self-esteem. Carl Jung believed that everyone, regardless of age, ability, education or culture instinctively understands personality in terms of these four colours, that we experience our humanness in these four colour dimensions.

Meaningful: ColourSpectrums will have a profound impact on your understanding of human nature. You will understand yourself better. You will understand other people better. ColourSpectrums will enhance your understanding of interpersonal and human dynamics. You will understand the concepts and be able to effectively apply them immediately in everyday life.

Painless: This won't hurt. We have a myth in our culture that the best way to learn about ourselves is to be dragged, kicking and screaming, through a painful experience; the greater the pain the greater the lesson learned. This is not true, and it is a "myth-understanding." While it is true that negative experiences are opportunities for personal growth, it is not necessary to inflict pain or create conflict in order to grow and develop personally. The fact is, when we feel anxious or threatened our defences go up; we resist change and retreat to the comfort and safety of old familiar habits. As a result our ability and potential to learn anything new is significantly diminished. ColourSpectrums workshops are presented in an atmosphere of mutual positive support that empowers participants, fosters personal growth, and promotes professional development.

Fun! ColourSpectrums workshops are presented to groups in a fun and entertaining workshop format that provides insights (aha! learning) and humour (ha-ha! learning). Research proves that laughter and learning go hand in hand. Laughter really is sound learning.

Long-lasting: You will remember and use ColourSpectrums for the rest of your life.

> I received a telephone call a few months ago from the human resources manager of a small prairie town in central Alberta. He asked me to present a ColourSpectrums workshop to the team of 30 town employees: receptionists, administrative staff, human resources personnel, department managers, supervisors, town council members and so on. I welcomed the opportunity to contribute to the team and alerted him to the fact that I had presented ColourSpectrums to the town employees five years earlier. He chuckled and explained what prompted his phone call. Over the past five years, there had been a significant turnover in staff due to cut backs, early retirements and a recent town election. The 10 current team members who had attended the workshop five years earlier were driving the newer staff members crazy with curiosity. "They keep talking about ColourSpectrums but we don't know what they are talking about." The workshop had only been three hours long, but the language of ColourSpectrums was still being actively used five years later in their day-to-day workplace environment. The ColourSpectrums concepts and applications you are about to learn will last your lifetime.

Introduction: What Is ColourSpectrums?

The History of ColourSpectrums

As human beings we have always been intrigued with the human experience. We have wondered who we are and pondered the questions:

"Who am I?"

"Who are you?"

"Why are some people so alike?"

"Why are some people so different?"

"Why do some people conflict?"

"Why do some people get along so well?"

Throughout human history and in cultures around the world, countless models have been created for understanding human behaviours and personality characteristics. One surprisingly common pattern has emerged. Human behaviours and personality characteristics have been repeatedly grouped into a pattern of four categories. We experience being human in four dimensions. This pattern of four is evident in the following examples.

Astrology

Astrology was one of the earliest attempts to explain similarities and differences in personalities. Astrology attributed the formation of personality to the external forces of the heavens. The 12 astrological signs were grouped into four categories, symbolized by the four "elements": water, air, fire and earth. It was believed that everything in the world was composed of some combination of these four basic elements.

The human body was also believed to be composed of these four elements. Each element was thought to have a particular influence on the personality. Excess water could dampen one's spirits. A person could be "full of hot air," have a "fiery personality," have a "hot temper" or temperature or be "down to earth." The familiar phrase "being in your element" is a reference to astrology. The phrase suggests that the situation you are in is a good fit for the kind of person you are. You can also be "out of your element."

Ancients and alchemists also used the four primary colours to represent the four elements: blue water, green air, red fire and yellow earth.

Hippocrates

In 400 B.C., the Greek physician Hippocrates, known as the father of modern medicine, explained personality as the combined influences of four bodily fluids. Each body fluid corresponded to one of the four elements: yellow bile (water), phlegm (air), red blood (fire), and black bile (earth).

Hippocrates referred to these body fluids as "humours," meaning moods. He contended that each humour had a particular influence on the personality, that each humour created a different mood. A person with a healthy balance of the four body fluids was said to be in a good "mood" or in good "humour." A person with an imbalance was "moody," in a "bad mood" or in "poor humour."

In medieval times, mood swings, mental illnesses and most diseases were believed to be caused by an imbalance of these four fluids.

Contrary to common belief, Hippocrates did not categorize people into four different types of personalities. He did not label or categorize people who had balanced personalities. He only used the terms choleric, phlegmatic, sanguine and melancholic to refer to <u>imbalanced</u> personalities.

Yellow bile created choleric attributes. Too much yellow bile was thought to cause anger, rage, fury, ire and wrath — a "bilious" personality. In medieval medicine a baby with these moody personality characteristics who cried and seemed angry was "colic," an adaptation of "choleric." The disease Cholera derived its name from choler (yellow bile.)

Phlegm caused phlegmatic characteristics. Too much phlegm caused a person to be indifferent, apathetic, unconcerned and unemotional. If you were listless and lethargic your body was thought to have too much phlegm resulting in an imbalanced phlegmatic personality.

Red blood had sanguine characteristics, meaning optimistic, cheerful, positive and upbeat. If you were overly optimistic, fanatical, hyperactive, frenetic or out of touch with reality, you were thought to have too much blood — a sanguine personality. Blood-letting and the application of leeches or blood suckers was based on the belief that relieving the body of excess blood could bring the personality back into balance. You can imagine what would happen to an overactive person after losing a couple of quarts of blood. The person would slow down, fall down or pass out. Blood-letting continued for centuries because it had the desired effect of slowing down hyperactive people.

Black bile had melancholic effects. Too much black bile caused a person to be sad, miserable, discontented, despondent, gloomy, forlorn and sorrowful. In this day and age…clinically depressed. If you were depressed, down in the dumps, or in a state of melancholy you were believed to have too much black bile — a melancholic personality.

On the surface it appears that Hippocrates' ancient thinking is outdated, not relevant in modern times. A closer look, however, reveals a basic underlying philosophy that holds great promise. Hippocrates was on to something. He believed that each body fluid had a specific influence, which meant that all four liquids and their four functions were essential to wellness and balance. Body fluids aside, the ColourSpectrums philosophy aligns with this same philosophy; each colour has a specific function so that a balanced influence of all four colours creates personal and professional balance and wellness.

Introduction: What Is ColourSpectrums?

The Medicine Wheel

The medicine wheel is another example of using the quartering of a circle and four colours. There are more medicine wheels laid out in stone patterns on the prairies in Alberta, Canada, than anywhere else in the world. Some of them are more than a kilometre across and date back more than 4500 years.

The four colours of the medicine wheel represent the four dimensions of human growth and development. While the colour combinations vary from one aboriginal nation to another, all medicine wheels consist of a combination of the four primary colours found abundantly in nature: blue, green, red and yellow as well as black and white.

Although the colours vary, the universal philosophy of the medicine wheel is constant: all four dimensions of human development are essential to wholeness. There are four seasons in a whole year: spring, summer, fall and winter. You can think of life as having four seasons: the spring (early spring — early childhood), the summer (mid summer — mid life), the fall and winter of life. The four seasons of life create the whole human experience. The use of the four cardinal points on the horizon and the four directions — south, west, east and north — to represent the human experience is a reflection of the close relationship that aboriginal people have had with mother earth. You must use all four directions to orient yourself geographically and metaphorically, to know where you have been, where you are, and where you are going.

It is astounding and significant that the medicine wheel, created on the opposite side of the planet and centuries removed from Hippocrates and the medieval world, uses the very same colours and four elements, the four elements observed in nature: water, wind (air), fire and earth.

Notably, the medicine wheel, which has evolved through centuries of broad cultural influence, does not categorize or label people the way that many models created by individuals do. Rather, the medicine wheel recognizes and values the balanced growth of all four dimensions essential to wholeness: emotional, mental, physical and spiritual development.

Carl Jung

In 1923, Dr. Carl Jung, the influential Swiss psychiatrist and founder of analytical psychology (1875 – 1961) wrote the book *Psychological Types*, in which he integrated the theories of Hippocrates, Plato and other ancient philosophers. Jung described four functions of consciousness and identified the four primary psychological energies in the psychic spectrum.

Jung associated each of the four functions of consciousness with one of the four primary colours. Jung described the feeling level of consciousness as a blue energy, the thinking level of consciousness as a green energy, physical consciousness as a red energy, and the intuitive/organizational level of consciousness as a yellow energy. Jung used a perfect geometrical grouping of four, a square or the quartering of a circle, to represent personal balance. These four primary psychological energies and colours in the psychic spectrum are the colours I use in ColourSpectrums. I chose these colours because I believe, as Jung believed, that all four energies are essential to wholeness, that all four energies are essential to balance. This is the ColourSpectrums philosophy.

Myers Briggs

Isabel Briggs-Myers and her daughter Katherine Briggs developed the Myers-Briggs Type Indicator. Based on the previous works of Carl Jung and others, this system classifies people into 16 different types with four groupings: Intuitive Feeler, Intuitive Thinker, Sensing Perceptor and Sensing Judger.

The History of Quadra Models

The grouping of human behaviours and characteristics into four categories dates back thousands of years and has many examples; five of these models and their historical classifications are listed below. The four categories of each model are aligned vertically to indicate similarities. Keep in mind that while there are many similarities, each model describes each of the four categories in different ways.

Yoga	Bhakti	Jnana	Karma	Raja
Hindu	Meaning	Success	Pleasure	Duty
Elements	Water	Air	Fire	Earth
Aristotle	Ethical	Dialectical	Hedonic	Proprietary
Islam	Blue	Green	Red	Yellow
	Terra	Aqua	Fuoco	Aria
	Earth	Water	Fire	Air

Quadra Models: One Common Theme, Two Different Philosophies

While all of these models have one common theme — the pattern of four categories — a closer examination reveals two basically different philosophies. Some models group people into four different categories. Some models describe all people as having four characteristics.

Quadra Models that Categorize People Into Four Groups

Some of the models that divide people into four different categories are listed below. Take note of the labelling language that is used for each of the four categories in these models.

Introduction: What Is ColourSpectrums?

For example:

Enneagram	Helper Romantic	Asserter Perfectionist	Adventurer Achiever	Peacemaker Observer
Plato	Philosopher	Scientist	Artisan	Guardian
Myers Briggs	Intuitive Feeler NF	Intuitive Thinker NT	Sensing Perceptor SP	Sensing Judger SJ
Keirsey	Idealist	Rational	Artisan	Guardian
Animals	Dolphins	Owls	Apes	Bears

Quadra Models that Describe Four Categories in all People

Some of the models that describe four categories as being in all people are listed below. Notice the descriptive language (rather than labelling language) that is used for each of the four functions in the following models.

For example:

Aboriginal	Emotional	Mental	Physical	Spiritual
Hindu	Meaning	Success	Pleasure	Duty
Jung	Blue Feeling	Green Thinking	Red Sensing	Yellow Intuiting
Dunn & Dunn	Emotional	Environmental	Physical	Sociological
ColourSpectrums	Emotional Blue	Intellectual Green	Physical Red	Organizational Yellow

ColourSpectrums belongs to this second philosophical group. Based solidly on Jungian philosophy, the four ColourSpectrums colours represent the developmental areas and functions of personality that everyone has.

ColourSpectrums

ColourSpectrums integrates and advances the knowledge, experience, research and wisdom of these and many other models. Based on Jungian philosophy, the four ColourSpectrums colours represent the developmental functions of personality that everyone has: blue emotional development, green intellectual development, red physical development and yellow organizational development.

You cannot be just one colour, be one "style," or be one "type." You cannot be categorized or labelled. ColourSpectrums does not use terms such as the "blue personality," "green personality," "red personality" or "yellow personality." Your ColourSpectrums personality and your human experience includes all four colours and each colour, regardless of whether it is bright or pale, has unique and significant implications.

Rather than labelling or categorizing people into different types as many models do, ColourSpectrums supports the understanding that everyone has, and uses, all four of these developmental functions in various combinations. While each function is distinct and separate, each person has natural abilities, preferences, learned behaviours, challenges and potentials associated with all four dimensions. ColourSpectrums is a developmental model that values everyone's unique blend of four colours and recognizes that your ColourSpectrums personality is continuously developing, growing and changing. All four colours play a vital role in who you are, how you are and how you are developing, growing and changing. Everyone uses all four functions simultaneously with varying combinations of intensity. Your particular blend of all four colours is your ColourSpectrums personality.

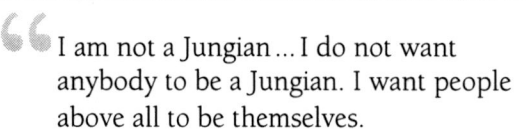

> I am not a Jungian... I do not want anybody to be a Jungian. I want people above all to be themselves.
>
> — Carl Jung

The History of Colours

Colours are such an important part of the human experience that every language in the world has words for colours. There are exactly 11 basic categories used throughout the world to describe colours. The 11 categories are listed below in the order that they are predictably added to languages.

The order of language development:

Primitive Languages	1) White 2) Black
More Developed Languages	3) Red 4) Yellow 5) Green 6) Blue
Well-Developed Languages	7) Brown 8) Purple 9) Pink 10) Orange 11) Grey

This order of language development is interesting from a global sociological perspective. From a more practical point of view it is significant because children's language development occurs in the very same order. Children first learn to recognize and name the colours "white" and "black." Then they learn "red," "yellow," "green," and "blue." Then they learn the other colours. ColourSpectrums' colours of blue, green, red and yellow are a great benefit when used with young children, people with learning barriers, people who are mentally challenged and participants who have English as a second language because these primary colours are more likely to be part of their vocabulary than colours such as orange or purple.

The Art of ColourSpectrums Colours

Leonardo da Vinci, Leon Battista Alberti and the other old masters used a practical colour system for mixing colours. They used the four primary colours: blue, green, red, and yellow, and used white and black to change intensities. These colours were not considered special because of any unique properties in the physics of light; rather, they were considered special because they corresponded to the natural sensitivities of the visual receptors in the human eye. Artists worldwide use these four primary colours to create diverse works of art. Using only these primary colours, artists can create all other colours. Similarly, we can use our palettes of four ColourSpectrums primary attributes to create diverse works of art: our diverse and unique personalities.

Artists have known for centuries that human perception of colour is dependent on the intensity of light. Greater intensity light causes the perception of orange and yellow-green to move towards yellow; violet and blue-green appear to become more blue as the intensity increases. Only blue, green, red and yellow are perceived as being independent of intensity, the only colours that retain their hue under changing lighting conditions. Artists like Leonardo da Vinci and the other old masters knew this and used only these four primary colours (plus black and white) so their works of art would not colour shift, would not change colour under changing lighting conditions when their works were displayed in different locations. That these works do not colour shift was only recently discovered by museum curators as they moved these famous paintings from one art gallery to another. The great masters' keen visual observations, that these primary colours do not colour shift, has now been scientifically proven.

Rob Chubb

The Science of ColourSpectrums Colours

The German physiologist Ewald Hering studied the human perception of colour from a more scientific perspective. He developed a theory that explained the fact that although our eyes have receptor cones for only three colours (blue, green and red), we actually see four primaries. His research concluded that yellow was not a mixture of red and green as suggested in the three-colour system of blue, green and red. He determined that yellow is elementary, and not traceable to a mixture. The colours blue, green, red and yellow are considered primary colours because each occurs without a perceived element of the other. Hering contends that all other perceived colours are a mixture of these four basic "psychological primaries."

The four ColourSpectrums primary colours are transmitted directly to the brain while other colours require further processing. Because these colours reach the brain faster in their pure form, the brain responds more quickly to these colours. The advantage of using these colours in ColourSpectrums workshops is that they have the highest possible recognition factor, are processed the most quickly and are absorbed at a deeper level in the brain. ColourSpectrums uses these colours to represent human functioning because they resonate naturally with human perception.

Section 1: Revealing Your ColourSpectrums Personality

Attribute Card Illustrations

Take out the four ColourSpectrums attribute cards. There are illustrations on one side of each card and written descriptions on the other side. Do not read the descriptions at this time. You will read them later and you will maximize this learning process if you suspend your curiosity for now. I am reluctant to tell people "not" to read the descriptions because you know what people are inclined to do when you tell them not to do something. Of course! They want to do it even more ... but bear with me. The wait will make the process more effective.

Right now you will be exploring the illustrations, one card at a time.

Emotional Blue Objects and Attributes

1) Refer to the blue objects and blue attributes workspace below.

2) Look at the illustrations on the blue card, write nine more objects seen on the card and beside each object, write a positive attribute you believe it represents. In the example provided the object is the "heart" and the attribute is "love." Remember to focus on positive human attributes.

Complete this list of 10 blue objects and attributes before reading further.

If you are working with a partner, write your lists separately, then share your impressions and compare your responses before reading further.

Rob Chubb

	Blue Objects	Blue Attributes
1)	*Heart*	*Love*
2)		
3)		
4)		
5)		
6)		
7)		
8)		
9)		
10)		

Emotional Blue Picture Elements

The blue illustrations can be interpreted in many different ways. There are no right or wrong impressions. The emotional and spiritual theme, however, is readily apparent. The illustrations depict the strengths, priorities, delights and talents of the blue attributes. The following detailed descriptions of each picture element will further your understanding.

Blue Objects	Blue Attributes
Artist's Palette	- artistic expression and creativity
	- inspiration and self-expression
Candle	- intimacy and romance
	- spiritual and prayerful
	- a guiding light
	- peaceful and calming
	- warmth
Cherub	- with his hand on his heart he offers the rose as if "giving from the heart"
	- his heart goes out to you
	- angelic
	- cupid is the cherub of love
Clouds	- dreaming and imagining
	- peaceful and calming
Daisy	- "she loves me, she loves me not"
	- "he loves me, he loves me not"
	- Do you like me? Do you love me?
	- our blue is sensitive to the state of personal relationships
	- beauty of nature

Section 1: Revealing Your ColourSpectrums Personality

Blue Dolphins	-	appear to be smiling, friendly and approachable
	-	socially interactive
	-	personally engaging communicators
	-	close, cooperative team work
	-	human beings have an affinity with dolphins
	-	dolphins are nature's most photographed creatures
Dove	-	the Greek symbol for love and peace
	-	the dove or love bird is the symbol of hope
Heart	-	the universally recognized symbol for love
	-	emotional energy is centered on the heart
	-	"heart" words refer to the blue attribute: warm hearted, kind hearted, heartfelt, heart-to-heart, broken hearted, from the heart, you melt my heart, my heart goes out to you and so on
	-	wearing your "heart on your sleeve"
Helping Hand	-	extending or lending a helping hand
	-	reaching out to provide personal or emotional support
Holding Hands	-	gentle physical touching is a natural expression of interpersonal relationships
	-	racial and ethnic diversity portrays mutual acceptance
	-	a genuine appreciation of human diversity
	-	strength in personal relationships
	-	standing together on the globe suggests "We are the world"
	-	we are all in this together
	-	love makes the world go around
	-	harmonious relationships and togetherness
	-	may the circle be unbroken
Music	-	being in harmony and rhythm with others
	-	music is the universal language that unites all people
Praying Hands	-	a universally recognized sign of prayer
	-	hands in prayer are centered over the heart
	-	worship and holy reflection
	-	spiritual, holy and prayerful reverence
	-	a sacred, spiritual and personal relationship with god
Rainbow	-	the awe-inspiring wondrous beauty of nature
	-	the sign of hope after a storm
	-	somewhere over the rainbow … skies are blue
Rose	-	love is a rose
Sky	-	blue skies mean smooth sailing
	-	hope and freedom
	-	all things spiritual and heavenly

Rob Chubb

Smiling Face	- friendly, kind, personable, approachable and welcoming
	- a warm smile is the universal sign of kindness, friendliness, openness and acceptance
	- when we are smiling we are getting along
	- smiling blocks the enzymes associated with fear
	- smiling reduces emotional tension and social anxiety
Sun/Moon	- the natural beauty of the rising and setting sun and moon
	- beauty and peace experienced in nature
	- the sense of awe and wonder
Water	- the calming, soothing rhythm of waves
	- deep blue emotional undercurrents
	- tides of emotions that ebb and flow
	- surging and turbulent oceans of emotions
	- the deep blue sea of emotions
	- waves of emotions
	- peaceful, calm and serene
	- life-giving water
Ying Yang	- balance, peace and harmony
	- the give and take shared in relationships
	- holistic approaches in which everything is interrelated and interdependent

Why Blue?

- The Earth is the blue planet teaming with life.
- Blue represents the harmonious relationships of all living things.
- The deep blue oceans reflect the depth of human emotions.
- Soothing sounds of blue ocean waves reflect calmness that words cannot express.
- Blue skies depict peace, harmony, hope and beauty.
- The celestial blue sky symbolizes the spirituality of all things heavenly.
- Blue attributes represent our personal relationships with each other, our relationship with ourselves and our spiritual relationship with god/creator.

Intellectual Green Objects and Attributes

1) Refer to the green objects and attributes workspace below.

2) Examine the illustrations on the green card, write nine more objects seen on the card and beside each object, write a strength you think it represents. In the example provided the object is Rodin's sculpture "The Thinker" and the attribute is "analytical." Remember to focus on positive qualities and strengths.

If you are working on your own, complete this list of 10 green objects and attributes before reading further.

Section 1: Revealing Your ColourSpectrums Personality

If you are working with a partner write your lists separately and then compare your responses and explain your ideas before reading further.

Green Objects	Green Attributes
1) The Thinker	Analytical
2)	
3)	
4)	
5)	
6)	
7)	
8)	
9)	
10)	

Intellectual Green Picture Elements

The green illustrations can be thought of in many different ways. There are no right or wrong interpretations. The cognitive and intellectual theme, however, is readily apparent. The illustrations depict the strengths, priorities, delights and talents of the green attributes. The following detailed descriptions of each picture element will further your understanding.

Green Objects	Green Attributes
Chess Pieces	- an intellectual game of strategy and wit
	- thinking ahead
	- a game played in the mind in thoughtful silence
	- contemplating endless possibilities and solutions
	- needing time to think things through
Compass	- measuring all angles with accurate precision
	- calculating and determining solutions
	- analyzing and problem solving
Dinosaur Bones	- the science of archeology uncovers, examines and unravels mysteries
	- digging meticulously beneath the surface
	- to explore, discover, make sense and explain
$E=MC^2$	- Einstein's mathematical equation and calculations explain the theory of relativity
	- Einstein put the pieces of the puzzle together to solve the mystery

	- Einstein is the icon for the green attribute
	- being scientific and mathematical
	- understanding and conceptualizing reality
	- devising and formulating solutions
	- mathematically inclined
Global Background	- contemplating a global perspective, a worldview
	- perceiving the big picture
Gyroscope	- the spinning gyroscope appears to defy laws of gravity
	- scientific principles of physics explain gyroscopic forces
Light Bulb	- a light bulb moment
	- when the light comes on
	- a bright idea or brilliant idea
	- to shed light on the matter
	- eureka! aha!
	- the experimental bulb represents technology
	- inventiveness, ingenuity, experimentation and innovation
Map	- a representation of reality
	- a conceptual model of the real word
	- exploring unknown worlds and endless possibilities
	- conceptualizing where we are and where we are going
	- measuring, calculating and navigating
Protractor	- to measure and calculate infinite angles with precision
	- analytical, mathematical and scientific solutions
	- calculating directions, determining solutions and plotting a logical course
Puzzle Pieces	- putting the pieces together to reveal the big picture
	- perceiving how pieces of information fit together
	- solving puzzles is a thoughtful, solitary process
	- observing, analyzing and conceptualizing relationships between ideas
	- solutions require meticulous inspection, observation, analysis and strategy
	- solving the puzzle requires a vision of the complete picture
Question Mark	- Who? What? Where? When? Why? How?
	- an inquisitive, curious mind full of endless questions and possibilities
	- the intrigue of unanswered questions
	- the mystery and intrigue of the unknown
	- What happened to the dinosaurs?

Section 1: Revealing Your ColourSpectrums Personality

Rubik's Cube	- an innovative invention, solitary activity and brain-teaser
	- mental competence of solving a puzzle on one's own
	- the solution requires mental concentration, analysis and complex problem solving strategies
	- think of the endless possibilities
	- there are 43 quintillion mathematical permutations (4.3×10^{10} = 43,252,003,274,489,856,000)
	- there is only one solution
Saturn and Stars	- the mystery of the rings intrigues the mind
	- scientific exploration and discovery of the unknown
	- space, a universe of infinite possibilities
Scientist/Researcher	- scrutinizing, analyzing, hypothesizing
	- technological know-how and scientific investigation
Test Tube	- testing ideas and theories
	- measurable, provable, quantifiable and experimental
	- hypothesis, experimentation and scientific observation
	- evidence, conclusions and new discoveries
The Thinker	- Rodin's classic sculpture is "The Thinker"
	- solitary contemplation and deliberation
	- in deep thought
Thought Bubble	- thoughts are central to this attribute
	- the binary code of zeros and ones is the mathematical language of computer-based data and information

Why Green?

- Why not?
- Green is abundant in nature.
- Green represents our curiosity to understand the nature of things.
- Green reflects the complex mysteries of earthly things, natural ecosystems, grasses and forests.
- Green is conceptual and scientific.
- Green is analytical and futuristic.
- Green attributes explore and promote new possibilities.
- Green has a calming effect and lowers blood pressure.
- Green searches for measurable, quantifiable, provable facts and data.

Rob Chubb

Physical Red Objects and Attributes

1) Refer to the red objects and attributes workspace below.

2) Have a quick look at the illustrations on the red card, then spontaneously write nine more objects seen on the card and beside each object, write a strength you think it represents. In the example provided the object is the "cheerleader" and the attribute is "enthusiasm." Remember to focus on positive qualities and strengths.

Complete this list of 10 red objects and attributes before reading further.

If you are working with a partner write your lists separately and then compare your responses and explain your ideas.

	Red Objects	Red Attributes
1)	The cheerleader	Enthusiasm
2)		
3)		
4)		
5)		
6)		
7)		
8)		
9)		
10)		

Physical Red Picture Elements

The red illustrations can be perceived in many different ways. While there are no right or wrong interpretations, the physical theme is readily apparent. The illustrations depict the strengths, priorities, delights and talents of the red attributes. The following detailed descriptions of each picture element will further your understanding.

Red Objects **Red Attributes**

Balloons
- light, buoyant and flamboyant
- fun-loving, playful and ready to party
- up in the air
- fun and playful

Basketball
- physical action and motion
- competition and winning
- physically skilled and talented
- sports and action oriented

Section 1: Revealing Your ColourSpectrums Personality

Bike Rider	-	physical courage and bravery
	-	winning
	-	risk taking dare devil
	-	gutsy, daring, death-defying feats
	-	dynamic, competitive and on the move
	-	nerves of steel
Checkered Flags	-	speed
	-	competition
	-	winning, thrilling
	-	loud and fast-paced
	-	high performance
	-	physical exhilaration and red rush of adrenalin
	-	pushing the limits
Cheerleader	-	motivation, enthusiasm and exuberance
	-	vigorous physical energy and excitement
	-	physically active, athletic, agile and nimble
	-	positive, upbeat, eager and resilient
	-	here and now
	-	pumped up and up in the air
	-	a good sport
Stage	-	on stage
	-	center of attention, centre stage
	-	live and in person
	-	dramatic performance
	-	risk taking
	-	stage presence
Curtain	-	What's behind the curtain?
	-	Surprise!
Exclamation Point	-	immediate impact
	-	emphatic and energetic
	-	exciting and dynamic
	-	spontaneous and bold
Kayaker	-	action packed physical adventure
	-	vigorous and competitive
	-	challenging rapids
	-	risk taking
	-	the adrenaline rush of living on the edge
	-	going with the flow and running the rapids
	-	moment to moment, non-stop action
	-	physical skills, balance and agility
	-	physically fit, strong, robust and able-bodied
Spotlight	-	the excitement of being in the spotlight
	-	the thrill of being on the spot
	-	You're on!
	-	being the centre of attention
	-	being in the limelight
	-	Lights, camera, action!

Rob Chubb

Thumbs Up/Coin Toss	- Give it a thumbs up!
	- everything is A-okay
	- it's "a go"
	- thumbing a ride or hitchhiking is physical, adventurous, risky, unpredictable and being on the move
	- Heads or tails? Take a chance or leave it to chance.
	- snap decisions, a flip of the coin, in the moment
Ultralight Plane	- freedom of action
	- high-flying adventure
	- flying over the hill and going over the top
	- ultralights are constructed and assembled by mechanically skillful mechanics
	- taking off, in search of novel experiences
	- up in the air, the sky is the limit
	- flying by the seat of one's pants
Wrench	- hands on
	- handy with tools
	- handy man, Mr. fix-it
	- Jack and Jill of all trades
	- mechanically inclined
	- a natural do-it-yourselfer
	- practical and adjustable
	- fixing, adjusting, repairing
	- being able to handle it

Why Red?

- Red is the colour of pulsing blood coursing through our bodies.
- Red is risk taking, physically active and thrill seeking.
- Red is transforming fire and heat.
- Red is bright, vibrant, eye-catching and attention getting.
- Red is pulsing, energetic and vigorous.
- Red catches our attention.
- Red is energetic, excited, sexual, urgent and immediate.

Section 1: Revealing Your ColourSpectrums Personality

Organizational Yellow Objects and Attributes

1) Refer to the yellow objects and attributes space below.

2) Look at each of the illustrations on the yellow card one at a time, write nine more objects seen on the card and beside each object write a strength you think it represents. In the example provided the object is the "boy scout" and the attribute is "prepared." Remember to stay on task and keep your attention focused on positive qualities and strengths.

Complete this list of 10 yellow objects and attributes before reading further.

If you are working with a partner write your lists separately and then take turns comparing your responses in an orderly manner.

Yellow Objects	Yellow Attributes
1) Boy Scout	Prepared
2)	
3)	
4)	
5)	
6)	
7)	
8)	
9)	
10)	

Organizational Yellow Picture Elements

The yellow illustrations can be perceived in many different ways. While there are no right or wrong interpretations, the organizational theme is readily apparent. The illustrations depict the strengths, priorities, delights and talents of the yellow attributes. The following detailed descriptions of each picture element will further your understanding.

Yellow Objects | Yellow Attributes

Accounting/Ledger Sheet
- being accountable and responsible
- budgeting, planning and controlling resources
- maintaining records and documenting proper procedures

Boy Scout
- the motto of this organization is "be prepared"
- keeping the promise to do your duty
- scout's honour
- a salute of respect and deference to authority
- boy scouts and girl guides are traditional institutions
- pride in being a member (in good standing) of an established organization
- established traditions, customs, rituals and procedural correctness
- uniforms promote uniform behaviour; uniformity
- fitting into a uniform helps you fit in
- badges of honour reward earned status and prestige in the organizational hierarchy
- being a responsible, solid citizen

Calendar
- Why is this date important? It's Canada Day.
- organizing, scheduling and arranging
- being orderly and planning ahead
- making commitments and being on time
- write it on your to-do-list
- write it in your planner
- write it on your calendar

Check Marks
- completing responsibilities in the right order
- checking to make sure tasks are completed correctly
- checking, double checking, and triple checking
- judging right from wrong
- judging correct and incorrect behaviours
- doing tasks the right way
- keeping things or people in check
- keeping track of duties, tasks and responsibilities

Coins
- saving
- preparing and planning for the future
- columns of coins suggest budgeting

Section 1: Revealing Your ColourSpectrums Personality

Fence	- establishing boundaries and setting limits
	- keeping things in
	- keeping things out
	- setting restrictions
	- establishing safety and security
File Folders	- maintaining records in order; chronological order, alphabetical order, numerical order or numerical sequence
	- keeping organized
	- following traditional and established office procedures
Flag	- being a loyal member
	- respect for authority and order
	- a symbol of national pride and allegiance
	- patriotic service, duty bound and honour bound
Block and Gavel	- order in the court
	- a court order
	- the rule of law
	- parliamentary procedures
	- rules of order
	- a time-honoured traditional symbol of law and order
	- to establish and maintain respect for formal proceedings
	- symbols of judgment and authority
	- symbols of the established system, the establishment, the government, law enforcement and formal powers that be
Gold Watch	- a traditional gift in honour of long-term commitment and dedicated service
	- time-management skills
	- time conscious
	- watch the time
	- being on time is being responsible
	- being punctual is being dependable
	- we organize ourselves by organizing our time
Hand Ringing Bell	- the school bell is a time-honoured tradition
	- time to get back to the task at hand
	- a symbol of authority and control
Highway	- following the straight and narrow
	- following the rules of the road
	- staying on the right side of the road
	- having a goal and direction
	- the road to success
	- you should not cross the solid yellow line

Rob Chubb

Money Background	- accumulating wealth, prestige, social status and possessions
Padlock	- the closed lock guards, controls and secures
	- having things locked up, locked down, safe, sound and secure
	- closure
Paper Clip	- keeping papers in order
	- paperwork maintains order and accountability
Pillars	- solid, straight, upright and traditional
	- pillars of society are solid, upstanding citizens
	- traditional symbols of the power of organizations and the strength of institutions: government buildings, court houses and banks
	- symbols of wealth
Pointing Finger & String	- focussing on the task at hand
	- pointing out details and tasks
	- a reminder to complete responsibilities
	- to tie up loose ends
	- completing tasks in order
	- one thing at a time
	- the judgment of a pointing finger
Service Bell	- ring for service
	- being of service

Why Yellow?

- The yellow sun is constant and dependable.
- The predictable patterns of sunrise and sunset establish daily routines.
- The daily, monthly and seasonal life cycles in nature follow the established cycles of the yellow sun.
- Yellow is stable, reliable, responsible and steadfast.
- Yellow is organized, traditional and prepared.
- Yellow is cautious, safe and stable.

Section 1: Revealing Your ColourSpectrums Personality

Completing the ColourSpectrums Scoring System

Use the ColourSpectrums attribute cards to complete the scoring system on the next page to reveal your unique ColourSpectrums personality. A completed example is provided for your reference.

If you are working with a partner, make a copy of the scoring system so you can each complete one. Discuss the results of each step before proceeding to the next step. In ColourSpectrums workshops participants work on their own to complete each step and at the end of each step they talk with a partner and take turns explaining why they arranged the illustrated cards and why they arranged the card descriptions in the order that they did. Talking and listening engages auditory and verbal processing. Dialogue enhances rapport and appreciation of diversity. Some participants like to talk more than listen while others like to listen more than talk. I encourage you to strike a balance when communicating with your partner. If you are a great talker, it may be at the expense of being a great listener so this is an opportunity to practise listening more. If you are a great listener, it may be at the expense of being an effective talker in which case this is an opportunity to practise talking (and so your partner can practise listening.) In either case, effective communicators can do both effectively. This is an opportunity to create an effective balanced dialogue with your partner.

ColourSpectrums™ Scoring System

1) Arrange the illustrated cards in order from your **most** natural to **least** natural attributes.
   Score the results in the innermost circle of the scoring area of the target at the bottom of this page as follows:
   Write a **4** in the quadrant that is **most** natural, then a **3**, a **2** and lastly a **1** in the quadrant that is **least** natural.

2) Turn the cards over and arrange the card descriptions in order from your **most** natural to **least** natural attributes.
   Score the results in the next outer circle of the target at the bottom of this page as follows:
   Write a **4** in the quadrant that is **most** natural, then a **3**, a **2** and lastly a **1** in the quadrant that is **least** natural.

3) Compare the top row of word pairs.
   Write a **4** in the box for the word pair that describes your **most** natural attributes, then a **3**, a **2** and lastly a **1** for the word pair that describes your **least** natural attributes.

   Do the same for all 6 horizontal rows.

AFFECTIONATE ARTISTIC	ANALYTICAL CONCEPTUAL	ADVENTUROUS DARING	CONSISTENT ECONOMICAL
CARING COMPASSIONATE	HYPOTHETICAL INTELLECTUAL	ENERGETIC EXCITING	ON TASK ON TIME
EMOTIONAL FRIENDLY	INTELLIGENT KNOWLEDGEABLE	FAST FUN-LOVING	NEAT ORDERLY
GENTLE GENUINE	LOGICAL OBJECTIVE	HANDS-ON IMMEDIATE	ORGANIZED PREDICTABLE
KIND-HEARTED LOVING	SCEPTICAL SCIENTIFIC	PHYSICAL SKILLED	PREPARED RESPONSIBLE
PERSONAL SPIRITUAL	STRATEGIC THEORETICAL	THRILLING UPBEAT	SCHEDULED TRADITIONAL

4) Add each column and write the totals here. →

5) Write a **4** under the highest total, a **3** under the second highest, a **2** then a **1** under the lowest. →
   If 2 columns are tied for the highest total, write 3.5 under both.
   If 2 columns are tied for the mid-range, write 2.5 under both.
   If 2 columns are tied for the lowest total, write 1.5 under both.

   Blue   **Green**   **Red**   **Yellow**

6) Write the scores of step 5 in the outermost circle of the corresponding quadrant of the target.

7) Add the numbers in each quadrant and write each total in the corner circle.

8) Your highest score is your brightest colour.
   Your second highest is your secondary colour.
   Your third highest is your third colour.
   Your lowest score is your palest colour.
   These four colours blend together to create your unique *ColourSpectrums* ™ personality.

   Blue   Green

   Red   Yellow

Copyright protected by *ColourSpectrums* ™
For use only with this book

Section 1: Revealing Your ColourSpectrums Personality

A sample of a completed scoring system.

Scoring System

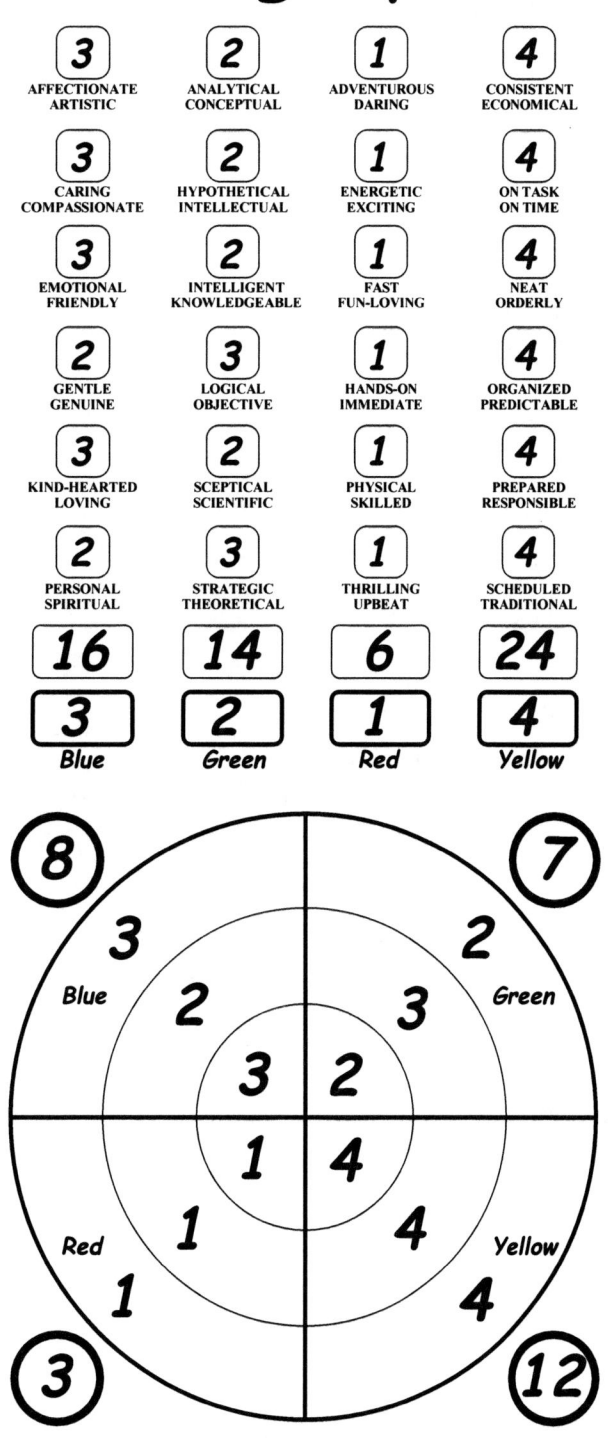

3	2	1	4
AFFECTIONATE ARTISTIC	ANALYTICAL CONCEPTUAL	ADVENTUROUS DARING	CONSISTENT ECONOMICAL
3	2	1	4
CARING COMPASSIONATE	HYPOTHETICAL INTELLECTUAL	ENERGETIC EXCITING	ON TASK ON TIME
3	2	1	4
EMOTIONAL FRIENDLY	INTELLIGENT KNOWLEDGEABLE	FAST FUN-LOVING	NEAT ORDERLY
2	3	1	4
GENTLE GENUINE	LOGICAL OBJECTIVE	HANDS-ON IMMEDIATE	ORGANIZED PREDICTABLE
3	2	1	4
KIND-HEARTED LOVING	SCEPTICAL SCIENTIFIC	PHYSICAL SKILLED	PREPARED RESPONSIBLE
2	3	1	4
PERSONAL SPIRITUAL	STRATEGIC THEORETICAL	THRILLING UPBEAT	SCHEDULED TRADITIONAL
16	14	6	24
3	2	1	4
Blue	Green	Red	Yellow

⑧ Blue 3, 2, 3 — Green 2, 3 ⑦
  inner: 3 | 2
  inner: 1 | 4
Red 1, 1 — Yellow 4, 4
③ ⑫

31

Reviewing the Results of the ColourSpectrums Scoring System

The final totals in each of the four corner circles represent your unique ColourSpectrums personality.

Your highest score is your brightest colour.

Your brightest colour is important. This is your primary source of esteem. These are the behaviours and characteristics you display the most often. You are familiar with these attributes and you identify closely with these behaviours and attributes. You have a reputation for using this colour.

Your second highest score is your second colour.

Your second colour is important. It is a secondary source of esteem. You are familiar with these attributes and display these behaviours somewhat less frequently and less intensely than your brightest colour. This colour blends with your brightest colour and modifies it. You identify with many of these characteristics and are quite proficient at using these behaviours. You are known for having many of these qualities.

Your third highest score is your third colour.

Your third colour is important. This colour is less esteeming for you. You are less familiar with these attributes and qualities. You use this colour less frequently and with less intensity. Some of these characteristics and behaviours are somewhat more challenging to use. You are perceived as not using this colour as intensely as your brighter ones.

Your lowest score is your palest colour.

Your palest colour is important. This is your least-esteeming colour. You are the least familiar with these attributes and you do not identify as closely with them. These are your least-developed behaviours and characteristics. You display them less often and less intensely. Just as you identify closely with using your brightest colour, you identify closely with not using this palest colour. Just as you are known for using your brightest colour, you are also known for not using this palest colour.

These four colours blend together to create your unique ColourSpectrums personality.

Arranging the cards in order from your most natural to least natural attributes does not mean arranging the cards in order of importance. Each colour plays an equally important but different role. Without being aware of it you may be unconsciously thinking that your brighter colours are more of who you are and your paler colours are less of who you are. This is not true. Your bright colours are how you are. Your pale colours are how you are not, which is how you are... (not).

> Because using a colour makes a difference, not using a colour makes a difference.

What you do and what you do not do are equally influential. It is the unique and personalized way in which you use and do not use these colours that is in fact your personality. It is the relative proportions of your colours that is your ColourSpectrums personality. Just as a single band of colour across the sky is not a rainbow, your personality is not one colour. You are not simply a "blue," "green," "red" or "yellow" person. Just as the old masters used these four primary colours to create their masterpieces, your ColourSpectrums personality is a unique multi-coloured canvas of four colours, a blend of contrasting bright and pale hues, bold and gentle strokes, brilliant and subtle shadings with diverse hues and an astonishing array of various tints and tones, a unique masterpiece.

> Your bright colours are how you are. Your pale colours are how you are not... which is how you are... (not).

The suggestion here on a metaphorical level is that you are the master of yourself. You are the artist in residence and you can use all four colours, all four of these functions to create your own masterpiece, your self-portrait.

The ColourSpectrums Scoring System: How and Why it Works

The ColourSpectrums scoring system is a unique process that stimulates and engages all of your colours. Understanding this process will further your understanding of how your colours function and how you determined your ColourSpectrums personality.

Sorting the Card Illustrations Stimulates and Engages Diverse Functions

The illustrations stimulate your blue emotional functioning. The pictorial representations, imagery, symbolism and illustrated metaphors elicit blue emotive responses and holistic impressions. To your blue a picture is worth a thousand words. You used your blue personal impressions to reflect on your sense of self to sort the illustrated cards. A positive emotive response suggests the colour's characteristics are naturally brighter for you. A neutral emotive response indicates the colour's characteristics are neutral, one of your middle colours. A negative emotional reaction to an illustrated card indicates the colour's characteristics are pale for you.

In ColourSpectrums workshops participants view animated presentations of each illustrated card. Each presentation is accompanied by a particular piece of classical music that creates a suitable mood. The blue animation is accompanied by Strauss's "The Blue Danube" waltz, green is accompanied by Beethoven's contemplative "Fur Elise," red is accompanied by Offenbach's upbeat "Can Can" and the yellow animation is accompanied by Sousa's traditional march "The Washington Post." The animations and music elicit deep intuitive experiences and rich underlying emotional associations.

Sharing these personal impressions with your partner also engages your blue.

Writing the objects and attributes engages your green intellectual functioning because it requires you to interpret the illustrations and put them into meaningful cognitive words. Explaining to your partner why you sorted the illustrations the way you did activates your green verbal functions as you put your thoughts into words and articulate your ideas.

Physically arranging the illustrated cards is a red hands-on kinesthetic activity that engages your red physical functioning. If your red tactile processing is bright, you couldn't wait to get your hands on them; you naturally took the cards in hand.

Arranging the illustrated cards in order is a yellow sequential activity that engages your yellow organizational function.

Sorting the Card Descriptions Stimulates and Engages Diverse Functions

Reading the descriptions on the reverse side of the cards is a more green cognitive process but it also engages all four of your colours' functions. Each "I" statement, strikes a chord with that corresponding colour in you. It is only your blue that can identify with the blue "I" statements. The brighter your blue is, the more closely your blue will identify with those statements. Only your green can identify with the green "I" statements so the brighter your green is, the more closely it identifies with those statements and so on.

Just as before, physically arranging the card descriptions activates your red physical tactile hands-on processing and arranging the card descriptions in order is an organizational activity that engages your yellow organizational functions.

Sharing your impressions with your partner engaged your blue and explaining this card sort to your partner engaged your green.

Sorting the Word Pairs

You used your green cognitive functions to sort the word pairs when you examined, studied, assessed, evaluated, quantified and rated them by assigning numerical values. You used your green to calculate your final scores.

Which Scoring Procedure Was Most Engaging?

In ColourSpectrums workshops I ask participants to indicate by a show of hands which of the following three sorting exercises they prefer. So, let me ask you. Which one do you prefer?

1) Sorting the illustrated cards
2) Sorting the card descriptions
3) Sorting the word pairs

Most participants prefer sorting the illustrated cards. Sorting the card descriptions is usually the second preference. The word sort is by far the least preferred. Even though it is usually the least preferred, least engaging and least meaningful process, the word sort is the method most commonly used by personality typing instruments and temperament tests. This stands to reason given that many personality style instruments are created by people who use their bright green

Section 1: Revealing Your ColourSpectrums Personality

cognition to conceive and design them. In their minds, human characteristics can be measured, quantified and categorized by an "instrument." This is not a balanced approach because it does not incorporate the blue, red and yellow influences, perspectives or learning processes. The ColourSpectrums scoring system engages all four processing functions. All of your colours are engaged in the process and influence the scoring results.

The Effects of Each Scoring Procedure

The ColourSpectrums scoring system stimulates different colours at different steps in the scoring process. The effects of stimulated colours can be observed at each step.

The illustrated cards and musically enhanced animations elicit strong emotions. Sorting the illustrations based on these holistic impressions is a blue process. As a result you may have scored your blue card higher when you sorted the illustrations.

Reading the card descriptions and sorting the cards based on those written descriptions is a more cognitive process. As a result you may have arranged the cards differently than when you arranged the cards based on the illustrations. If two cards switched positions it suggests those two colours are fairly equal in strength. If so, you may use one colour or the other interchangeably or use them together depending on the situation:

1) You may use one of the colours more intensely because it is more effective or appropriate in a particular situation.

2) You may use one colour more intensely for a while, and as it becomes saturated or fatigued you use it less and use the other colour more, relieving one colour and reviving the other.

3) When colours are equal in strength you may use them together in a blended combination. I describe these paired collaborations in Book 3.

Both card sorts are physical hands-on exercises that stimulate red hands-on tactile learning functions. Participants who have red as a brighter colour sort them quickly and can't wait to move on to the next exercise. If your red is bright you may have scored your red higher when physically sorting the cards than when sorting the word pairs.

Sorting the Word Pairs

When workshop participants sort the illustrated cards they have a natural tendency to talk to each other and share their impressions. I encourage this natural learning process because it engages visual, language, verbal and auditory processing. Each of these functions occurs in different regions of the brain. Using them all simultaneously integrates the learning experience.

When participants read and sort the card descriptions they talk less because the region of the brain that processes reading and the meanings of words becomes occupied (or preoccupied, if you will).

When participants sort the word pairs the talking stops. Communication stops because the word sort is a solitary green process that requires the green mind to analyze word pairs and assign mathematical values. When the green mind is occupied with these mental functions it cannot simultaneously process and articulate other words required for conversation.

The ColourSpectrums Scoring System: A Transparent Process for Everyone

This scoring system is a self-scoring, transparent process. Nothing is hidden. It is not mysterious. You can see how the scoring is being calculated as you proceed. Your ColourSpectrums results are about you, so it simply makes sense that you are actively aware and fully engaged in the process. This engagement empowers you to take ownership in the process and invest in the results.

After the word pairs are ranked, the column totals are assigned weighted values of 4, 3, 2 or 1. This conversion gives the word pairing exercise the same weighted value as each of the two preceding card sort exercises. This places equal value on each of the three scoring processes: card illustrations, card descriptions and word pairs. Most importantly, this places equal value on all four colours so that all of your four colours influence the final results.

Observations about Card Sorting and Word Pairing

When instructed to sort the illustrations, workshop participants frequently ask what criteria they should use to sort them. "Should I arrange them according to how I am at work, how I am at home, the way I used to be, the way I want to be, and so on?"

> We are so busy adapting to the demands of a fast-paced, hectic life style that we may not be sure who we are. We become "human doings" rather than "human beings."

If you have been under a great deal of stress lately you may have difficulty arranging the cards or word pairs in your naturally esteeming order. The process of sorting the cards and word pairs is a process of self-reflection in which you tune into your natural sense of balance, what is more or less naturally empowering. When you are under stress you are not in an empowered state, you are not in a naturally balanced state, and you are not in tune with your natural sources of self-esteem. If you are experiencing high levels of stress the criteria for sorting the cards can be confusing. You might wonder if you should sort the cards according to who you "should be," "could be," "used to be," "have to be," "try to be, " "want to be," and so on. In other words you may not be in touch with your true balanced self. If so, keep reading. You've come to the right book.

We expend a great deal of energy adapting our behaviours so we are effective in diverse situations. We have a spectrum of behaviours: a persona we use at home, another spectrum of behaviours that we use at work, another spectrum of behaviours that we use at school or with friends or in the community and so on. The fact is, our spectrum of behaviours is continuously changing from one moment to the next. We respond to different people and different situations in different ways.

We are constantly and necessarily adapting our ColourSpectrums because we need to be effective, fully functioning human beings in diverse situations. It is difficult to sort the cards when you cannot differentiate between your adapted behaviours and your natural behaviours. Interestingly enough, children usually sort the cards more quickly and decisively than adults. A child's internal experience (who they are) is naturally more congruent with their behaviours (how they are). With children... what you see is what you get. Their behaviour does not change much from one situation to another, much to the dismay of parents at times. Infants and young children tend to behave the same way in church as they do on the playground. They behave the same way at home as they do at the grocery store. Oh to be as congruent as a child... once again.

The key to the ColourSpectrums scoring system is to focus on what is more and less "natural" and arrange the card illustrations and card descriptions and rank the word pairs in order from your most natural to least natural attributes.

ColourSpectrums will help you get back in touch with your true self and reclaim who you truly are so you can be yourself, rather than being beside yourself. If you find it difficult to put the cards in order, simply... let it go for now, give this process time and revisit it later. It may have taken a long time to get out of touch with yourself, so it may take some time to get back in touch and experience personal congruence.

> A few years ago, I had the privilege of presenting ColourSpectrums to a group of 20 older teens at the Boys and Girls Club in Jasper, Alberta. We were at a rustic retreat centre nestled in the spectacular Canadian Rocky Mountains. The young people were all actively participating except for one young man who was somewhat withdrawn and seemingly detached. When he sorted his cards I noticed he placed his blue card as his palest colour at the end of the table. During the break we all walked over to the camp kitchen for refreshments. I made a point of sitting at the same table as this young man in the hopes of connecting with him. At an opportune moment I asked him how long blue had been his palest colour. His eyes welled up in tears. "Ever since my aunt died last year," he confided. As he told his story it became evident that his blue was hurting and in emotional pain. As a foster child he had been moved numerous times from foster home to foster home until an aunt took him in to live with her. He had been living with her for about four years, when she suddenly died in a car accident the previous year. He hadn't placed the blue card as his palest colour because it was. He placed the blue card as his palest colour because he felt out of touch with his blue — because his blue needs for love, affection and a deep sense of personal belonging were not being met. In the grieving process of death and loss, he was feeling depressed, detached from his blue emotions.

Rob Chubb

Circle Blend

This next activity will help you integrate the four colours of your ColourSpectrums personality. It is an opportunity to reflect on your overall colour blend by "drawing" on your self-awareness.

A Visualization Exercise: Imagining Your Best Balance

Imagine having a great week in which you experience all four of your colours in ways that are most comfortable for you. Visualize how you would use your blue to satisfy emotional needs for relationship, love and affection. How would you experience your blue in just the right proportions, not too much blue and not too little? How would you use your green? Think about how much green you would want to satisfy your intellectual need to analyze, think, understand and ponder the possibilities. How would you use your red and how much red would you want to experience to satisfy your red needs for physical activity, action and excitement — not too much red activity and not too little, just the right amount for you? How would you use your yellow? Imagine having a great week in which you experience just the right amount of yellow to satisfy your need for control, routine, structure, planning and organization. Keep in mind (that would be a green "think" to do) that some of your needs get met at work, some of your needs get met at home and some of your needs get met in other situations. What would a great week look like if you experienced all four of your colours in the proportions that seemed best for you?

To colour the circle on the next page use four crayons or felt pens (blue, green, red and yellow) to create a visual representation of how you would use your colours in a balanced week. If you haven't had a great week lately, just imagine the possibilities. This is an opportunity to visualize one. If you are working with a partner make a copy of the circle and complete this step of the exercise separately.

Section 1: Revealing Your ColourSpectrums Personality

ColourSpectrums™ Circle Blend

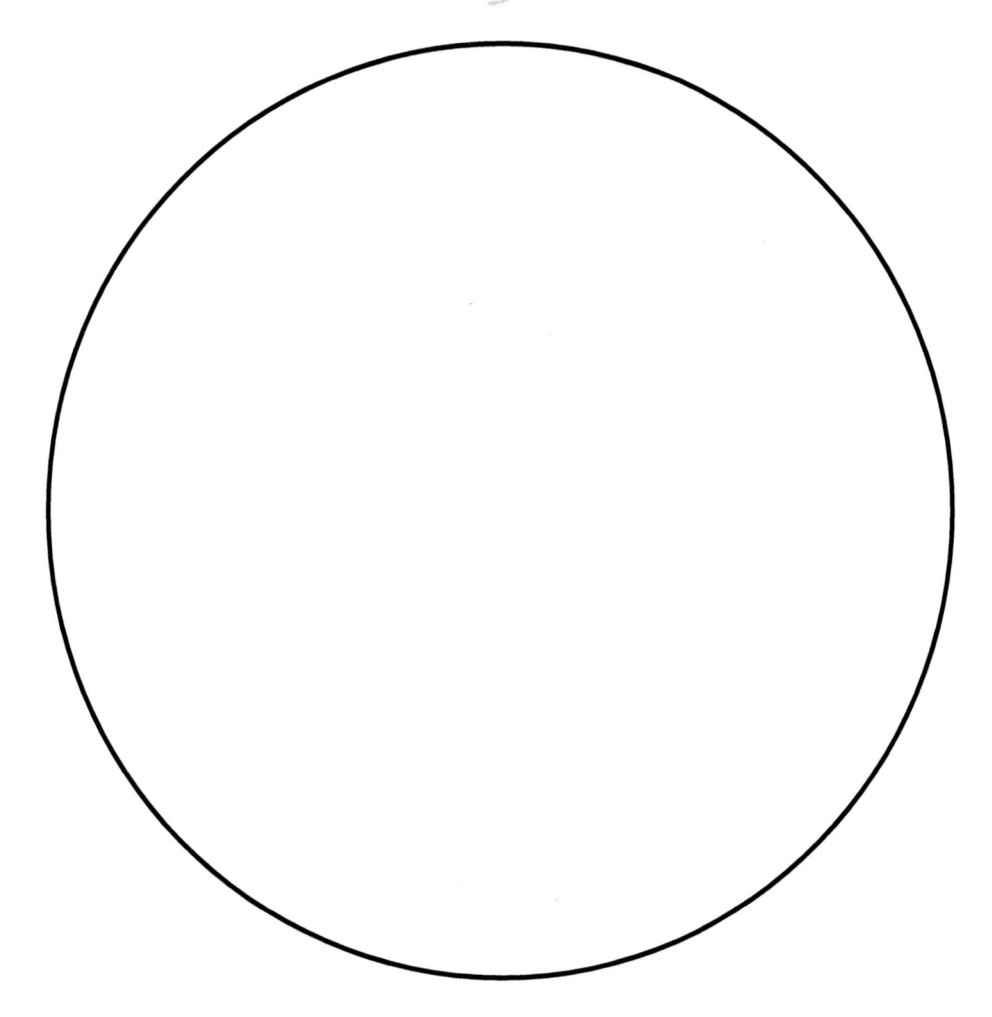

Describe your circle blend to your partner.

Take turns describing your circles to each other. Describe your great week and give specific examples of how you like to experience and satisfy each of your colour's needs. Listen attentively, ask questions and learn what is important to your partner. What does balance mean to him or her. How does your partner experience balance?

How do your colours influence how you complete this task?

Thousands of workshop participants have completed this circle blend exercise. Participants' ColourSpectrums influence how they approach and complete this task. Consider how your colour spectrum influenced you by answering the following questions.

1) How did you use your two brightest colour functions to complete this exercise?

2) How did you not use your two palest colour functions to complete this exercise?

As you read the following descriptions of how others have completed this circle blend exercise, consider how you used your two brightest colours and how you did not use your two palest colours. Each of the following descriptions focuses on one colour at a time. The reality is that all four of your colours had a simultaneous but different influence, your brighter colours influencing what you did and your paler colours influencing what you did not do.

Blue Circle Blends

Participants with blue as their brightest colour begin by using the colour blue first. They perceive this exercise as an opportunity for self-expression. They follow their intuition and go with their feelings rather than referring to their actual scoring results. Participants with bright blue talk to others about their great week, sharing personal stories and anecdotes as they colour their circles. They imagine the circle is their personal canvas and approach the exercise with artistic flair. They personalize and humanize their illustrations by drawing people and depicting interpersonal interactions. They draw people-friendly environments full of life — scenes with houses, grass, trees, flowers, sunshine, clouds, rainbows, birds, butterflies and other living things that personify their lifestyle. Pastel colours are blended together with gentle shadings and smooth transitions from one colour to another. Drawings include circular shapes, ovals, rounded corners, curves, wavy lines and soft edges. If your blue is bright, then you probably used these techniques to colour your circle to give it a certain feeling or overall emotional impression. If your blue is pale, then you probably did not use these approaches. As a result your circle may have a certain appearance because it does not have these elements.

Green Circle Blends

People with green as a brightest colour think of this exercise as a problem to be precisely analyzed and accurately solved. They analyze the scoring system and are naturally sceptical of the validity of the scoring results. They are strategic and conduct research by referring to the scoring system to calculate and quantify precise proportions. Visualize a group of 30 instructors at the Northern Alberta Institute of Technology completing this exercise. I watched with intrigue as seven instructors with bright green pulled out calculators (yes they had them close by) to convert their raw scoring results to πr^2 to calculate precise pie chart percentages for each colour. Using the value of Pi for a pie chart; who would have ever thought? Precision and accuracy matter when you use green. The instructors put their heads together and consulted each other. While other participants perceived a simple, uncomplicated, straightforward exercise, these participants were intrigued by the complexities they detected. It piqued their curiosity. While people with bright blue perceive the wholeness of a circle, people with bright green perceive a pie chart. They use pens, pencils, rulers, and protractors to design the chart. They measure precisely and divide the circle into four sections to conceive the main idea. Once they think it through they use a green felt pen or crayon to colour each segment. They use geometric designs. They sketch or draw each portion of the pie chart and frequently colour some of it in just enough to get their point across. On occasion they write the names of the colours instead of actually colouring them. This green approach is more of an analysis of the scoring results than a process of self-reflection or self-expression. Once their green has figured it out and conceived the main ideas, the interest and intrigue rapidly wanes. If your green is bright then you likely used these techniques. If your green is pale, then you were probably not interested in these strategies and they would not have crossed your mind or even come to mind.

Red Circle Blends

Participants who have red as their brightest colour view this exercise as an activity, as an opportunity to do something and take action. They can't wait to get started. They begin quickly while the verbal instructions are still being given. They get excited and quickly grasp handfuls of felt pens. They start colouring with red and scribble impulsively with bold strokes, streaks and flamboyant flare. To these participants the area within the circle is just a suggestion, an approximate drawing space that is too small. Their playful, enthusiastic colouring bursts over the edge without regrets or apologies. They sketch large, bold pointed shapes like stars and arrows and triangles with sharp edges. They draw zigzags, stripes, cross-hatched lines and splashes of colour to add attention getting, eye-catching flare, zest, pizzazz and chutzpah! Sports symbols and action figures predominate. They start first and finish first and then move quickly to other activities. They can been seen sniffing the felt pens or stacking them end to end and dueling with the resulting sword-like props just for something to do...and the red part of us is always on the go, looking out for something to do. These playful participants use the felt pens to decorate their body parts such as arms, faces and hands. Sometimes they colour each other. They are often caught red-handed and red-faced! If your red is bright, you likely took some of these courses of action. If your red is pale then you probably didn't use many of these behaviours. The absence of these red qualities will affect the overall look of your circle.

Yellow Circle Blends

Participants who have yellow as their brightest colour take this task seriously. Firstly, they listen intently to all of the directions so they can do it the right way. Secondly, they raise their hands to clarify the details of the directions so they can adhere to the proper procedures. They want the directions spelled out to the letter and follow the directions to a "T." They dot the "i's" and cross the "t's" and mind their "p's" and "q's." Then, and only then, do they proceed to the third step, the task of colouring the circle. As with most people they start colouring with their brightest colour so they begin with yellow. They check the scoring system to make sure they follow the results and complete the task the "right" way. They use rulers or straight edges to draw traditional pie shapes. They pay meticulous attention to organizational details. The felt pens or crayons are carefully controlled with straight edges. The divisions are cautiously aligned and separated, the colours are solid, evenly coloured and do not go over the lines. They perceive that there is a right way and a wrong way to complete the task. When they judge that they have made a mistake they ask for a new worksheet so they can start over and do it right. Neatness counts. They draw traditional symbols and arrange them symmetrically and evenly spaced on the page. The end result is a planned and orderly drawing with clearly separated colours. It is uncluttered, symmetrical and balanced. They complete the task in a responsible manner and take pride in the professional looking results. The yellow part of us takes pride in completing tasks properly. How did you use your yellow in this exercise. If your yellow is bright you will have followed these procedures. If yellow is one of your paler colours you probably did not adhere to these yellow procedures when completing this task. As a result your circle may not have these qualities and that will affect the look of your circle.

Consider how you approached and completed the circle blend exercise. What did you do? What did you not do? What you did affects the look of your circle. What you did not do affects the look of your circle. This self-awareness can provide you with a window of insight on how you approach many tasks in life. A slice of bread tells you a great deal about the rest of the loaf. Understanding this slice of life — how you completed this exercise — can reveal a great deal about how you approach many other situations in life.

> How you do this, is how you do everything.

Unique Circle Blends

In ColourSpectrums workshops, participants are asked to hold up their coloured circles so everyone can see them. They are then instructed to find someone who has coloured the circle the same way. The variety of coloured circles is astounding and while some participants find circles that look similar, no one ever finds an identical one.

Participants are then given a second challenge. They are instructed to find someone who has a circle that is different from their own. As you can imagine, participants don't have to look very hard to find someone with a different circle. As it turns out... every circle is unique.

The point is, that while everyone uses all four colours, no two people use these colours the same way. Your great week, for example, is not the same as anyone else's great week. You have a unique combination of needs that must be satisfied in personally meaningful ways. You have colours that must be experienced in just the right proportions. No one uses these colours with the same intensities and combinations that you do. Every person has a unique ColourSpectrums personality.

Section 1: Revealing Your ColourSpectrums Personality

ColourSpectrums Day-to-Day

In the spaces below, write examples of how you use your colours day-to-day.

Refer to ColourSpectrums attribute cards for ideas and write everyday examples. If you are working with a partner, make a copy of this page and complete the written exercise separately.

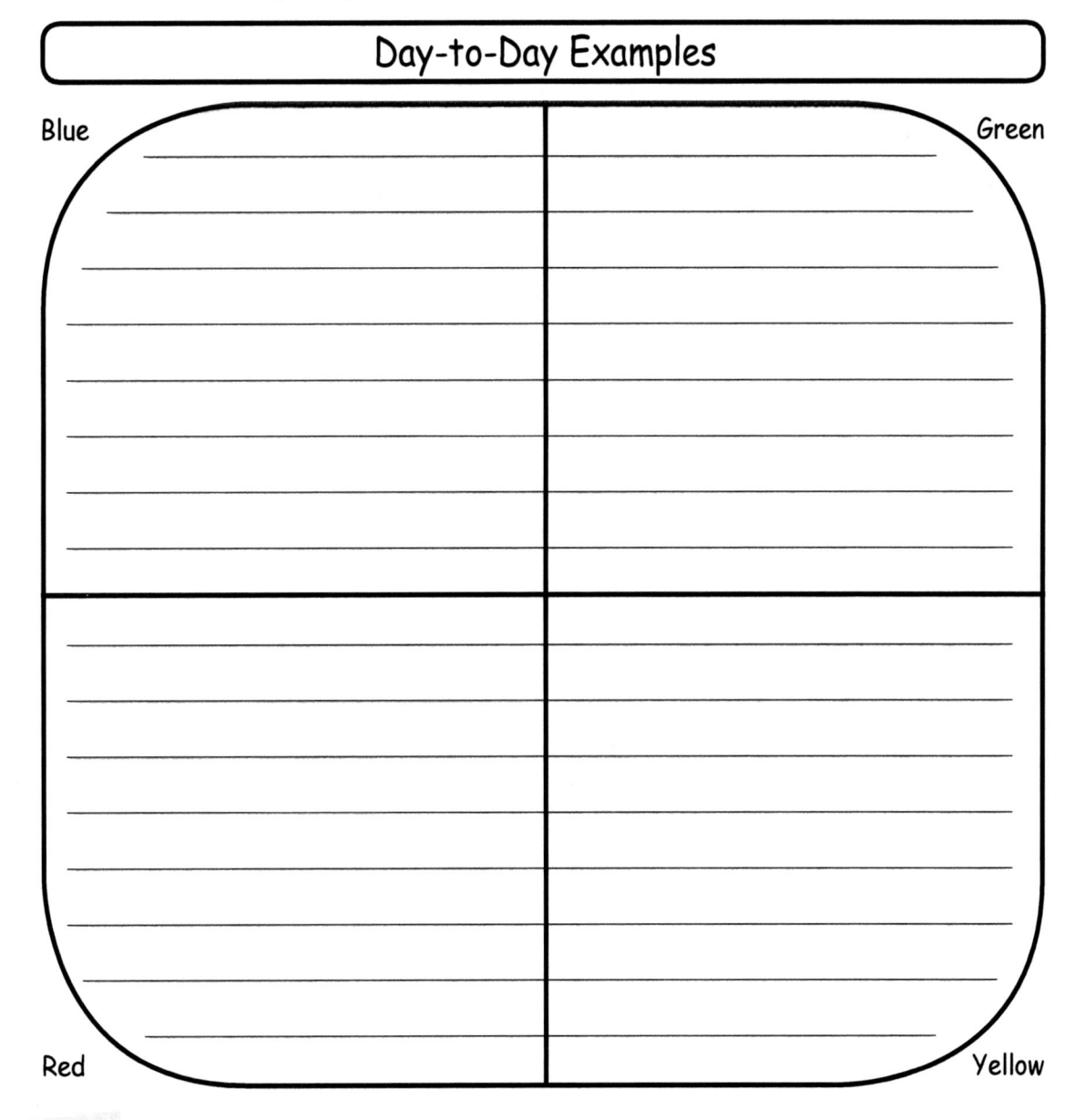

Day-to-Day Examples

Blue | Green

Red | Yellow

Talk With Your Partner

When you and your partner have completed this written exercise individually, share the results with each other.

Rob Chubb

Displaying Your ColourSpectrums Personality

Your ColourSpectrums personality is represented by four coloured circles in vertical order:

The top circle represents your brightest colour.

The second circle represents your second colour.

The third circle represents your third colour.

The bottom circle represents your palest colour.

Review the colour spectrums illustrated below and colour the appropriate one.

If each of your colours has different values, colour this spectrum.

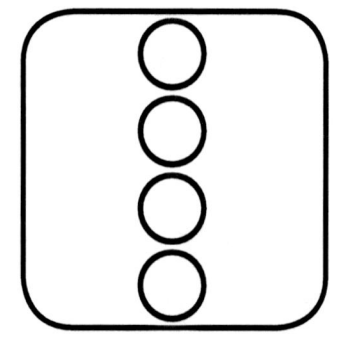

If two of your colours have equal values, colour the spectrum below that matches yours.

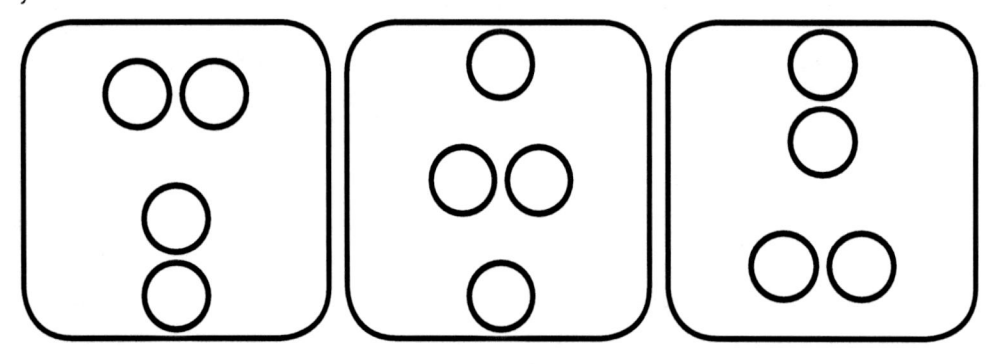

Section 1: Revealing Your ColourSpectrums Personality

If two of your colours have equally bright values and two of your colours have equally pale values, colour the following colour spectrum.

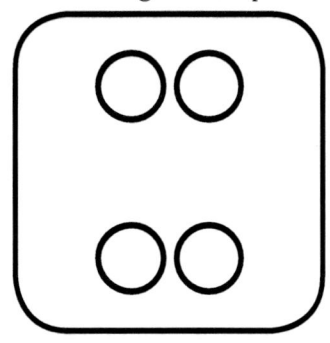

If three of your colours are equally bright, colour the spectrum below.

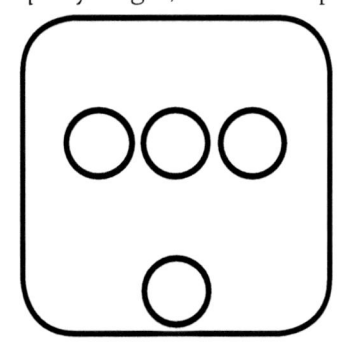

If three of your colours are equally pale, colour the spectrum below.

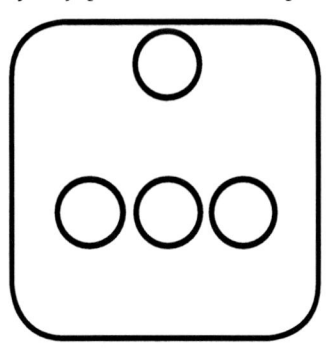

If your four colours have equal values, colour the following colour spectrum.

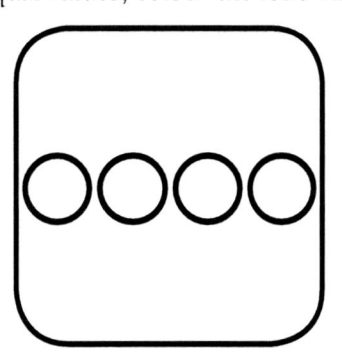

Rob Chubb

Section 2: ColourSpectrums Implications for You and Others

Picture yourself in a ColourSpectrums workshop with 30 participants who are milling around the room and interacting. Everyone is wearing name tags with four colour dots that display their colour spectrums. Your task is to get together with everyone else who has the same colour spectrum as you. How many people do you think you could find who have the same ColourSpectrums personality as you?

How Many ColourSpectrums Are There?

How many different ordered combinations of these colours are possible? Take a few minutes to consider this question and write your answer in the space provided before reading further.

How many colour spectrums are possible? _____

In the same way that your colour spectrum influenced how you coloured in the circle in the colour blend exercise, your colour spectrum also influences how you respond to this question. Participants in ColourSpectrums workshops are asked the same question. When the question is asked, participants are wearing name tags with colour dots that indicate their ColourSpectrums personality. As a result, it is easy to determine the influences of their brightest and palest colours as they respond to this question.

As you read the following behavioural descriptions, consider how your brighter colours influenced what you did in response to the question and consider how your paler colours influenced what you did not do.

Participants who have blue as a brightest colour begin talking with people around them. They share their hunches, impressions and gut feelings as if they have a sixth sense about the number of possibilities. They encourage participants to agree and to reach a group consensus. If someone believes there are about 16 combinations and someone else has the impression there are around 24 combinations, the person with bright blue diplomatically suggests a compromise, encouraging participants to reach a group consensus of about 20 possibilities. When pressed for an answer they remain undecided, accepting and accommodating a flexible range of possibilities.

Rob Chubb

Participants who have green as a brightest colour are intrigued by the question. The range of possibilities piques their interest. They begin by thinking about it. When they have independently thought it through as far as they possibly can on their own, they consult with others. They use mental math or write mathematical equations and formulas to calculate accurate solutions. They use calculators to ensure accuracy and precision. Their solution is often based on the mathematical formula for calculating combinations and permutations. (That mathematical equation is 4 x 3 x 2 x 1 = 24). They would rather figure out the answer on their own or get a hint before being given the actual answer.

Participants with red as a brightest colour lead with their actions. They quickly pick up the cards and hold them in their hands. They physically shuffle and reshuffle the cards to see what happens. They move the cards randomly to create various combinations to see what they can come up with. This engages their physical, tactile, hands-on learning. When asked for an answer they quickly quip, "There are lots!"

Participants who have yellow as a brightest colour clarify the task and then rely on their innate sense of order to get the right answer. They write lists of sequential colour combinations to determine all the possible ordered sequences. Their lists look like this:

blue	blue	blue	blue	
green	green	red	red	
red	yellow	green	yellow	
yellow	red	yellow	green	and so on.

This approach is systematical, but not mathematical. If their red is also bright they will use their red and yellow by picking up the cards, taking them in their hands and physically rearranging the cards in various ordered combinations.

So what is the answer? More accurately... what are the answers?

How many ColourSpectrums are there?

1) There are 24 ColourSpectrums that have four different colour intensities. The formula for calculating these combinations and permutations is
   (4 x 3 x 2 x 1 = 24)

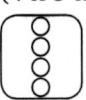

	1	2	3	4	5	6	7	8	9	10	11	12
Brightest	B	B	B	B	B	B	G	G	G	G	G	G
Second	G	G	R	R	Y	Y	B	B	R	R	Y	Y
Third	R	Y	G	Y	G	R	R	Y	B	Y	B	R
Palest	Y	R	Y	G	R	G	Y	R	Y	B	R	B

Section 2: ColourSpectrums Implications for You and Others

	13	14	15	16	17	18	19	20	21	22	23	24
Brightest	R	R	R	R	R	R	Y	Y	Y	Y	Y	Y
Second	B	B	G	G	Y	Y	B	B	G	G	R	R
Third	G	Y	Y	B	B	G	G	R	R	B	B	G
Palest	Y	G	B	Y	G	B	R	G	B	R	G	B

2) There are 12 ColourSpectrums that have two colours as brightest colours.

	1	2	3	4	5	6	7	8	9	10	11	12
Brightest	BG	BG	BR	BR	BY	BY	GR	GR	GY	GY	RY	RY
Third	R	Y	G	Y	G	R	Y	B	B	R	B	G
Palest	Y	R	Y	G	R	G	B	Y	R	B	G	B

3) There are 12 ColourSpectrums that have two colours as middle colours.

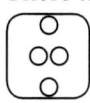

	1	2	3	4	5	6	7	8	9	10	11	12
Brightest	R	Y	G	Y	G	R	B	Y	B	R	B	G
Middle	BG	BG	BR	BR	BY	BY	GR	GR	GY	GY	RY	RY
Palest	Y	R	Y	G	R	G	Y	B	R	B	G	B

4) There are 12 ColourSpectrums that have two colours as palest colours.

	1	2	3	4	5	6	7	8	9	10	11	12
Brightest	R	Y	G	Y	G	R	B	Y	B	R	B	G
Second	Y	R	Y	G	R	G	Y	B	R	B	G	B
Palest	BG	BG	BR	BR	BY	BY	GR	GR	GY	GY	RY	RY

5) There are 6 ColourSpectrums that have two colours as brightest colours with two colours as palest colours.

	1	2	3	4	5	6
Brightest	BG	BR	BY	GR	GY	RY
Palest	RY	GY	GR	BY	BR	BG

6) There are four ColourSpectrums that have three colours as brightest colours.

	1	2	3	4
Brightest	BGR	BGY	BRY	GRY
Palest	Y	R	G	B

7) There are four ColourSpectrums that have three colours as palest colours.

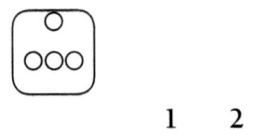

	1	2	3	4
Brightest	Y	R	G	B
Palest	BGR	BGY	BRY	GRY

8) Only 1 of the ColourSpectrums has four colours of equal intensity.

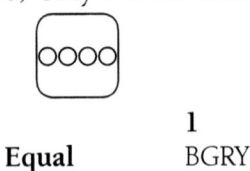

	1
Equal	BGRY

Mathematically there are 75 ColourSpectrums

The ColourSpectrums cards can be arranged in 75 ordered combinations:
(24 + 12 + 12 + 12 + 6 + 4 + 4 + 1 = 75)

In addition to these 75 ordered combinations there are three levels of scoring in each quadrant that range from a low of 3 points to a high of 12 points so that each of the 75 ColourSpectrums has many various combinations of proportions. When all of the mathematical proportions are calculated there are **over 5,000** possible combinations.

The point is that ColourSpectrums uses four primary colours to represent four easily understood attributes that can be combined in thousands of possible ordered combinations and various proportions. Someone who has the same order of colours as you will have them in different proportions. In addition, our colour spectrums change. In a workshop with 30 participants you would probably find only one or two people who have the same colour spectrum as you and those people would use their colours in different proportions. Everyone has a unique ColourSpectrums personality.

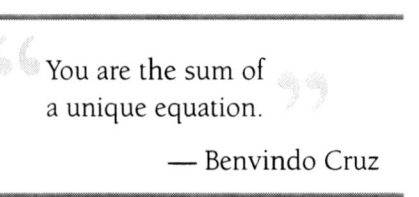

> " You are the sum of a unique equation. "
>
> — Benvindo Cruz

Section 2: ColourSpectrums Implications for You and Others

Knowing what someone's colour spectrum is provides significant insights. It does not, however, tell you how the person is using their colours at any given moment... and how someone uses their colours when interacting and communicating is what is most important.

So, while ColourSpectrums may appear simplistic on the surface, the underlying complexities are profound.

> ColourSpectrums is complex but not complicated.

Reflections From Brisbane

ColourSpectrums is so easy that a four-year-old can understand it.

A couple of years ago I presented ColourSpectrums at a foster parent conference in Brisbane, Australia. One of the foster mothers approached me the next day and excitedly told me what happened when she returned home following the workshop. When she arrived home she set the ColourSpectrums cards on the kitchen table and when she came back to the kitchen her 4-year-old foster daughter was sitting at the kitchen table looking at the illustrated cards.

Her foster daughter had been living with the foster family for three months and was in foster care because she had been emotionally neglected and physically abused. She was extremely shy and withdrawn. The girl looked up at her mom and asked, "What are the cards for?" The mother, seeing the opportunity to dialogue with her daughter, responded, "These cards are about the kind of person you are." The mother and daughter explored the illustrations and discussed each card. On her own initiative, the young girl asked if she could give the cards names. She looked at the blue card and said in a soft, kind and friendly voice, "That's the friendship card." She studied the green card for a moment and stated, matter-of-factly "That's the thinking card." She took the red card in her hands and enthusiastically announced, "This is the fun card!" When she looked at the yellow card, she sat up straight and with a serious look and a stern voice said, "This is the work card."

The foster mother asked the daughter, "Which card is most like you?" The daughter sorted through the cards, picked up the yellow card and said firmly, "I am a work girl."

The mother asked her how she was a "work" kind of person. The daughter described her morning routine, how she liked to get up at the same time every morning, make her bed and fluff her pillow. She liked to hang her clothes in her closet, line up her shoes side-by-side on the floor and organize and straighten up the books on her bookshelf. She routinely vacuumed her room twice a day. Her mom explained to me that this girl had the neatest, cleanest room in the house. In fact, every evening like clockwork, before getting tucked safe and sound into bed this little girl would get the clothes she planned to wear the next day — her shirt, her pants, her underwear, her shoes and her socks — and neatly arrange them in order on her dresser.

Rob Chubb

> The mother and I gave each other a knowing glance as we suddenly realized the significance of her organizational and ritualistic behaviours. This girl had been in an environment of abuse, neglect and chaos, in an environment that lacked boundaries and controls. Given a set of four ColourSpectrums cards, 10 minutes, and a listening ear, this little girl was able to describe exactly what she needed: the comfort and security of a safe, predictable environment and the ability to establish boundaries and exert control.

Brightest Colour Presentations

In ColourSpectrums workshops, participants are divided into brightest colour groups to prepare and present group presentations that educate the other participants about the priorities, delights and talents of using their brightest colour. During this exercise participants are considered to be the experts on their brightest colour. They are the most familiar with it because they use it most often and with the greatest intensity.

The reality is that everyone uses all four colours simultaneously with varying intensities. For this exercise, however, participants are instructed to suspend their three paler colours as much as possible and focus on using only their brightest colour. This is a challenging task because second colours are just below the surface and usually have a significant influence.

This brightening exercise provides participants with the opportunity to experience their brightest colours with greater intensity than usual. This proves to be an esteeming and empowering experience in which participants celebrate the strengths of each colour, one at a time, and ultimately celebrate the diversity of all four colours.

Each brightest colour group is provided with a tickle trunk of props for use in their presentations. Props include costumes, shirts, pants, hats, scarves, gloves, shoes and so on. Participants are also encouraged to use other resources such as flip charts and music.

Groups are instructed to consider a variety of presentation formats including skits, role plays, formal presentations, songs, lectures and discussions. They are encouraged to choose a presentation format that is the most natural for them and that reflects the natural style of the colour they are presenting. Participants are encouraged to be creative, to be insightful, to have fun or to be serious...whatever it takes to educate the rest of the participants about the priorities, delights and talents of using their brightest colour.

Brightest Colour Preparations

Usually when we interact in a group, different people use different colours with various intensities. As a result we tend to modify our own colours and intensities in order to interact effectively with different people. We don't often have the

Section 2: ColourSpectrums Implications for You and Others

opportunity to interact with a group of people who are all using the same colour. In ColourSpectrums workshops this exercise gives participants a unique opportunity to experience a group dynamic in which everyone in their group uses the same colour; in this case, the same brightest colour. This is a rare treat. As participants interact their brightest colours are mutually reinforced and those colours become brighter and brighter as a result. Participants using blue experience their blue more intensely, participants using green, red and yellow experience their brightest colours more intensely. This brightening process is an esteeming, validating and empowering experience. By the time participants are ready to make their group presentations their brightest colours are intense and they are ready to present their brightest colours with confidence, pride and clarity.

Brightest Blue Preparation

> Let us observe and listen in on a group of six workshop participants who have blue as their brightest colour as they prepare a presentation on the priorities, delights and talents of using their bright blue attributes. What behaviours would you expect to see and what would you expect to hear?

Participants who have blue as a brightest colour naturally tune in to each other's blue; they are highly responsive to each other's personal presence. They accommodate each other, kindly offer each other chairs, and take care to ensure everyone feels comfortable. They position themselves around the table in such a way that they can see each other, make eye contact, and facilitate effective interpersonal communication. They sit close together. They use first names to introduce themselves in a warm, welcoming and friendly manner. These well-wishers interact on a personable level. They warm up quickly to each other and have a gift for creating genuine personal rapport. It appears as if they genuinely wish to be friends by being friendly and "befriending" each other. They look for friendly faces in a crowd, yet have the power to befriend strangers. Their communication creates a sense of community spirit. These are relationship-oriented people and people come first. Relationship building is their first priority. They get to know each other on a first name basis before attending to the task. If there is more than one group with blue as a brightest colour, those groups often join together to form one large cohesive group. These participants gather around and sit close together, pressing shoulder to shoulder. Their heads and shoulders lean forward creating feelings of closeness, togetherness and inclusion that enhance rapport and interpersonal dialogue. It appears as if they are getting together for a social gathering or a "get-together." They display random acts of kindness as they attend closely to each other. They take great care to include everyone in the discussion and engage every person in the process. They are more interested in "getting along" than "getting the task done." Decisions are reached by consensus meaning that everyone has a say, is listened to and agrees to "go along to get along." These amicable participants are personally engaging, friendly and kind. They are keenly aware of personal space and frequently apologize for interrupting or bumping into each other. Minor disagreements and discord are rare and short lived. They are quick to offer the olive branch of peace and goodwill. They value interpersonal communication and accommodation. They share creative inspirations. These cordial, good-natured participants display a natural gift for relating personally and for creating a genuine sense of group cohesion and team spirit.

Brightest Green Preparation

These participants display autonomy and independence. They sit apart from each other and appear aloof and detached. Introductions are not a priority. They read through the handout materials and sit in thoughtful silence as they integrate the information and ponder the possibilities. These participants are more interested in relating and attaching to ideas than relating and attaching to each other, more interested in knowing than in knowing each other. They engage in active debates as they try to get their points across. They challenge each other's ideas, question each other's assumptions and put their ideas to the test. They spend a great deal of time clarifying terms and definitions. They dispute and debate the meanings of the words "priorities," "delights," and "talents." They define their own terms and search for precise terminology that makes more sense to them. In other words, they are interested in other words. Contemplating meanings is intellectually meaningful. For these participants debating, deliberating and redefining terms are mentally stimulating processes that engage their intellectual and cognitive functioning. Deliberations are intriguing, interesting and absorbing mental exercises that facilitate the integration of new information. Debating stimulates the formulation of new ideas and the exploration of innovative possibilities. As these participants explain their ideas and articulate individual points of view they take more pride in delineating differences of opinion and establishing autonomous thought than in establishing a common understanding.

> Now let us observe and listen in on a group of six workshop participants who have green as their brightest colour. They are strategizing and preparing a presentation on the priorities, delights and talents of using their bright green attributes. What behaviours would you expect to see and what would you expect to hear?

Brightest Red Preparation

This is by far the loudest and most physically active group. They often attract the attention of others. They often distract the attention of others. These lively, boisterous participants are energized by what they perceive as a lucky break to perform in front of a live audience. Introductions are jovial, playful exchanges with high fives. Rather than talking about what to present, these participants move quickly into action. They impulsively root through the box of props in a flurry of activity and can't wait to get their hands on them. They spontaneously try on various costumes. They use the props to improvise and act out impromptu skits for each other to see what catches each other's attention. They are like a barrel full of monkeys having a barrel full of laughs — flamboyant, fun-loving, playful and full of beans. As they get more excited, they become increasingly animated, frequently standing up and moving around the room. Their energy is contagious and rises rapidly in a beehive of activity as they make a bee line for the door and race headlong out of the room to find a staging area where they run through their performance; then, lickity split, they are back in a flash in a whirlwind of excitement. This group of actors looks like they are having a party. They have a field day! They are ready first, revved up and raring to go on stage. They are a travelling road show and can't wait to get the show on the road. If they have to wait they get restless. If the anticipation of presenting wears off and their initial excitement wanes, they reenergize themselves by quickly moving on to another, more novel presentation that reignites their excitement. They are ready to act on a moment's notice and they end up presenting whatever activity they are "playing" with when they are called upon to present.

> Let us observe and listen in on a group of six workshop participants who have red as their brightest colour as they prepare a presentation on the priorities, delights and talents of using their bright red attributes. What behaviours would you expect to see and what would you expect to hear?

Section 2: ColourSpectrums Implications for You and Others

> Let us observe and listen in on a group of six workshop participants who have yellow as their brightest colour as they organize a presentation on the priorities, delights and talents of using their bright yellow attributes. What behaviours would you expect to see and what would you expect to hear?

Brightest Yellow Preparation

This group takes the task seriously. These participants begin in a traditional manner with formal salutations and customary handshakes. They establish roles early by using last names, formal job titles and positions. They frequently refer to the organizations they work for. In contrast with the participants who have blue as a brightest colour who appear to be having an informal gathering, get-together, or reunion, this group looks like they are taking care of business and they get down to business as if conducting a formal businesslike meeting. While people with bright blue see themselves as working with people, people with bright yellow see themselves as working for an organization. These participants conduct themselves in a serious, professional, businesslike manner. They prepare for the work ahead by clearing their table of clutter. They arrange the remaining work-related items to create an orderly workspace. They straighten up everything. They straighten up the table, they straighten up their chairs, they straighten up their posture and sit up straight. They take out pens and lined paper and prepare to take notes as if recording the minutes of a formal meeting. They write notes while people with bright red jot notes, and people with bright green make mental notes. They listen attentively to all the verbal instructions first. Then they read the written directions thoroughly to check and double check the details. They raise their hands to check on procedures that are not clearly spelled out. They clarify the task with questions such as, "How much time do we have to prepare?" "How long is the presentation supposed to be?" "Should we use a flipchart?" These participants are intent on following detailed directions so they can complete the task properly. Getting the detailed directions straight is the first step in doing it right. They are more interested in clarifying procedures than in clarifying content. This bright yellow group is concerned about being properly prepared and completing the task correctly. Organization is the order of the day. They often use a conventional flipchart to prepare their presentation in advance. The use of the flipchart provides structure to their discussion. The person writing the list of items in order on the flipchart has the powerful effect of establishing order and controlling the discussions so that the group focuses on one task at a time. This formalizes the proceedings and establishes a tone of professionalism. One or two participants take charge of the group by assigning roles, delegating responsibilities, and establishing procedures. The use of props is planned ahead of time and their use is closely controlled so they are used appropriately in the right order at the correct time.

Priorities, Delights and Talents

We have joined a ColourSpectrums workshop in progress. Let us continue watching and listening as the brightest colour groups make their presentations. If the colour being presented is your brightest colour, you will identify closely with the presenters and their priorities, delights and talents. If the colour being presented is your second colour you will also identify with those presenters because that colour is just under the surface for you. If the colour being presented is your palest colour... pay attention! That is the colour that you understand the least of all and potentially have the most to learn about. This can be your greatest learning opportunity.

Rob Chubb

Brightest Blue Presentations

The group that has blue as a brightest colour begins their presentation by gathering closely together in a group at the front of the room. These participants are conscious of self and sometimes report being self-conscious about presenting. If one of them is overly self-conscious or reluctant to present, other group members are quick to notice and respond intuitively by offering personal encouragement and supportive gestures. These presenters personalize their experience by wearing the props and getting into roles. They identify personally with the props and perceive them as extensions of themselves, expressions of who they are. They stand in a circle or semi-circle so they can see each other's faces, make frequent eye contact and respond interpersonally. They smile often. They are naturally comfortable with close physical proximity and touch each other frequently — shoulder to shoulder, hand-in-hand, arm-in-arm, and with arms around each other's shoulders and waists. They take care to accommodate and include everyone. No one feels left out as they share the stage. Leadership is undefined. Their positive group spirit and sense of mutual support flows naturally from person to person, emanating from a collective consciousness. Frequent nodding and verbal agreement encourages mutual support and acceptance. Participants frequently complete each other's statements as if what is being said is commonly agreed, agreeable and acceptable. These presenters personalize their presentation. They identify personally with the priorities, delights and talents of using their blue and they reveal their experiences by revealing themselves to the audience. They present personal narratives, human interest stories and anecdotes. They role play personal experiences to portray their priorities, delights and talents. The presentations are humanized and include many "I," "us," and "we" statements. They use poetry and music to express themselves.
It is natural for these participants to share their experiences with others so these presentations are experiential. They encourage audience participation by singing songs that everyone is familiar with and they encourage the audience to join in and sing along. They prefer to sing with people than sing for people. They would rather gather a close circle of friends around a campfire and sing folk songs. "Sing-a-longs" create group harmony, literally and figuratively. Blue energy is holistic and circular; it is represented in the round yin and yang symbol of balance and is part of healing circles. Group hugs are a natural expression of genuine companionship. They believe what goes around comes around. When this group has finished presenting I thank them for putting their hearts into their presentation and for the opportunity to get to know them better. The audience uses their blue to give these presenters an appreciative, genuine, heartfelt thanks and warm round of applause.

Bright Blue

Priorities

emotions	empathy	friendship
genuineness	harmony	kindness
love	people	personal growth
relationships	self-esteem	spirituality

Delights

acceptance	being together	belonging
bonding	companionship	empathizing
fellowship	getting along	helping
intimacy	relating	self-discovery

Talents

artistic	authenticity	benevolent
caring	cooperative	empathic
encouraging	expressive	inspirational
interpersonal	people skills	rapport

Brightest Green Presentations

Inclined to be sceptical, this group may resist or be reluctant to present if they haven't had time to think it over and make sense of the information. Because one of their primary sources of self-esteem is to be knowledgeable and "to know," their greatest fear is appearing as if they don't know what they are talking about. If they can't make sense of the exercise and don't get the point they don't see the point in presenting. As they walk to the front of the room to make their presentation it becomes apparent that they are solitary individuals rather than one cohesive group. They take pride in being independent thinkers, and they stand apart from each other at the front of the room. They prefer a no-nonsense approach and seem largely indifferent to the props, which they usually do not wear. They occasionally pick them up and use them to explain or demonstrate ideas or concepts. Then they set them back down. These presenters use words to articulate their priorities, delights and talents. When one of them explains an idea, he or she will unconsciously step forward and stand apart from the others as if detaching and emphasizing their standalone, independent, autonomous perspective. When they are finished explaining their ideas they step back. Instead of one cohesive group presentation, these individuals actually make four or five individual, solitary presentations. They take pride in having a mind of their own. They have to make up their own mind (but don't take my word for it). They actively and openly debate, disagree, concur and challenge each other's ideas in front of the audience as one thought leads to another. They are contemplative, pensive and value original thought, more interested in getting ideas than in getting along. These presenters are articulate, using highly developed vocabulary with confidence. They choose their words and terminology precisely to convey accurate meanings. They are lucid and they elucidate. They use big words... like "elucidate" (if you know what I mean). They can be sesquipedalian (yup... given to using long words). They verbalize their conscious stream of thought and sound as if they are thinking out loud as their train of thought switches from one track to another. They use flip charts to draw mind maps, models and diagrams to explain their ideas and to get their points across. They talk about their ideas but not about themselves. Focused on ideas, they intellectualize most of their discussions. They value mental stimulation and often solicit questions from the audience. This is a strategic way of getting the audience to think, to use more of their green. Questions from the audience keep the presenters intellectually stimulated and mentally active. These presenters respond confidently to the questions and value these opportunities to elaborate, expound and enlighten the audience.

When this group has finished presenting I thank them for their concise articulation, eloquence, and innovative ideas. Their green appreciates being valued for being knowledgeable, insightful and profound. We use our green to give a thoughtful round of applause, applauding them for their great ideas, food for thought, hindsight, insight, and foresight.

Bright Green

Priorities

data	evidence	explanations
facts	ideas	independence
information	logic	objectivity
research	science	strategy

Delights

analyzing	autonomy	conceptualizing
explaining	figuring out	independent thought
inventing	investigating	new ideas
solving	thinking	time to think

Talents

analytical	articulate	formulating
independent	innovative	knowledgeable
matter-of-fact	objective	observant
strategic	tough-minded	visionary

Brightest Red Presentations

The group that has red as a brightest colour jumps at the chance to perform before a live audience. They just can't wait to stand up and stand out! They are Johnny on the spot and good to go. Chomping at the bit and ready for action, they parade to the front of the room with fanfare as they burst onto their imaginary stage and jockey for position at centre stage. It's show time! While other participants see the front of the room as a place to make a group presentation, these presenters perceive a stage and a chance to shine in the spotlight, a thrilling and exciting unexpected opportunity to perform live. For these go-getters, actions speak louder than words. They lead with their actions and improvise action-packed spontaneous presentations. These presentations look and sound like a three-ring circus with a variety of improv performances happening simultaneously and in rapid succession. Like perpetual motion machines they have nonstop dynamism as they feed off each other's contagious high energy. These eager beavers rub their hands together in eager anticipation and use props enthusiastically. They perform upbeat skits and present action-packed role plays and entertain with all the theatrics of a variety show. They wing it and make it up as they go along. It can be a free for all but they can swing it. They take the task lightly and use slapstick comedy, practical jokes and animated behaviours to keep their presentations lively and entertaining. They jazz it up! They ham it up! These presenters use loud, upbeat music and energize their audience with showmanship, razzle dazzle, flamboyance, panache and flair! Their happy-go-lucky attitude is contagious. They need room to move and move freely through the open spaces in the room. This group gets a kick out of evoking boisterous audience reactions, bursts of laughter and spontaneous applause. They take great delight in being prized for their fun and exciting performances. They are hands down the most entertaining and put on a great show. We use our physical red to stand up and put our hands together to clap and give this group an outrageous, thunderous, rowdy, boisterous, enthusiastic standing ovation!!! They react enthusiastically to a curtain call. You gotta hand it to them; they can't be upstaged and are a hard act to follow.

Bright Red

Priorities

action	courage	daring
fun-loving	hands-on	here and now
humour	living on the edge	physical movement
risk-taking	spontaneity	thrill-seeking

Delights

activity	adventure	competing
entertaining	improvising	performing
risking	speeding	testing limits
touching	variety	winging it

Talents

courageous	dynamic	energetic
enthusiastic	flexible	improvising
multitasking	physical	positive
resilient	self-starters	upbeat

Brightest Yellow Group Presentations

The participants who have yellow as a brightest colour are orderly and walk to the front of the room in single file. They can be heard organizing the details of their planned presentation and finalizing arrangements as they prepare at the front of the room. They perceive the room as a formal classroom or business setting and assume their role at the front of the room as a position of authority. They accept the responsibility to teach the audience about their priorities, delights and talents. They stand up straight and line up straight, side by side, in a prearranged sequence according to their assigned roles and responsibilities. Everyone has a proper place. They usually line up in the order in which they plan to present each of their assigned tasks. Sometimes they stand in order according to height, age, seniority or other organizational criteria. They establish order by waiting for the audience to "settle down" and "pay attention" before starting. They firmly hold papers and pens and are well prepared to make a formal presentation. Everyone in this group is ready with an ordered list of points to cover. Each person has written the same list, as if someone used a copying machine. This ensures that everyone knows what everyone else's job is. The presentation is orderly because each member has a pre-assigned or delegated role. They often use three prepared flipcharts, one for each of the three major headings: 1) priorities, 2) delights, 3) talents. Each major heading contains subheadings with details in order of priority. Predictably one presenter reads the list of priorities, a second presenter reads the list of delights and a third presenter reads the list of talents. They stick to their agenda and follow the timelines given for the presentation. They instruct the audience to hold their questions until their formal presentation has been completed. During the question period they direct audience members to raise their hands, wait their turns and be given formal permission before asking a question. These formalities ensure that questions can be answered one at a time in an orderly, controlled and structured format. This group takes pride in their work and a job properly done; they are proud of a well-prepared, organized and orderly presentation. This is the only group that brings closure to their presentation with a clearly defined ending. We give this group a traditional formal round of applause. Their yellow appreciates the respect they receive for attending to organizational details and for completing the assigned task according to the directions in a responsible, professional and timely manner.

Bright Yellow

Priorities

being a member	details	duty
institutions	loyalty	order
organizations	responsibility	routine
standards	tasks	tradition

Delights

arranging	being in charge	being of service
being on time	being prepared	being responsible
completing tasks	earned status	earned rewards
organizing	planning	saving

Section 2: ColourSpectrums Implications for You and Others

Talents

consistency	coordinating	dependable
disciplined	economical	follow through
hard working	prepared	punctual
reliable	scheduling	steadfast

The brightest colour presentations provide participants with an opportunity to experience their brightest colours with brilliant intensity. This experience is personally validating and empowering. Diverse colours are celebrated.

Debriefing Brightest Colour Presentations

The brightest colour presentations provide a glimpse into rarely seen human behaviour, the opportunity to observe a group of people using the same colour with bright intensity. As much as possible each group uses only their brightest colour. The group presenting blue only uses blue, the group presenting green only uses green, the group presenting red only uses their red and the group presenting yellow only uses yellow. Understanding these colours one at a time in their primary forms is the key to understanding them in their more usual paler and blended forms.

It is important to keep in mind that these presentations call for participants to focus only on their brightest colour. In reality everyone uses all four colours simultaneously all the time with varying intensities. On the surface it appears that a person's brightest colour is more important than a person's paler colours. Nothing could be further from the truth. You will discover that all of your colours, regardless of the order in your ColourSpectrums personality, have equally profound and different implications. If using a colour makes a difference, then not using a colour makes a difference.

> Using a colour has implications...
>
> So not using a colour has implications.

Following the brightest colour group presentations, participants take a moment to detach themselves from their intense brightest colour experiences by visualizing the presence of their other three colours. This helps participants reintegrate their ColourSpectrums. Participants also take a moment to appreciate that everyone, regardless of their brightest colours, uses all four colours with varying intensities. This de-roling helps participants acknowledge and appreciate all four of their own colours and to appreciate all four colours that everyone else has. De-roling also minimizes the risk of labelling people as a colour.

The point is, you are not a colour! As tempting as it is to label people, it is critical not to. Do not refer to yourself or someone else as a "colour." Saying, "I am a blue" or "you are a green" is not helpful (and not true). A person cannot simply be a "blue" person, a "green" person, a "red" person, or a "yellow" person. When we label anyone we put them in a box. We are saying that they have the same attributes as everyone else who is in the same box. Even though you have the same brightest colour as many other people, you do not have all of the same qualities of your brightest colour. The way you use your brightest colour is different than the way other people use the same brightest colour.

> You are not a colour.

Knowing that someone has the same brightest colour as you tells you nothing about how bright or pale the person's other colours are. Simplistic labelling and typecasting devalues people by diminishing the importance of their other colours, by diminishing the uniqueness of their ColourSpectrums personality.

When ColourSpectrums participants work in brightest colour groups they realize they have a lot in common with participants who are in the same group because they do have the same brightest colour. In ColourSpectrums workshops participants also work in palest colours groups on other tasks. When they do they realize that they have just as much in common with those group members because they have the same palest colour... and they are different people because their brightest colours can different.

Categorizing and labelling people according to their brightest colours makes no more sense than categorizing and labelling people according to their palest colours. Unfortunately many personality style models simplistically label people according to their stronger qualities and ignore all the other characteristics.

It is human nature to group, categorize, and label people. Even before you were born people wanted to know which category you were in. They asked your parent(s), "Are you expecting a boy or a girl?" When you were born it's the first thing anyone wanted to know. While a person can be categorized as a boy or a girl, a man or a woman, a Caucasian person, an aboriginal person, a black person, or an Asian person and so on, none of those categories or labels tells you anything about the individual person. Categorizing and labelling is seductive because it is easy, convenient, simplistic and believable and yet none of it is true for the individual because it disregards individual uniqueness.

In ColourSpectrums workshops I jokingly ask participants to indicate, by a show of hands, if they would like to be categorized or labelled. The response to this rhetorical question of course is a swift, predictable and resounding, "No!" But when I ask participants if they would like a quick and convenient way to categorize and label other people they humorously admit that would be awesome. The proliferation of personality typing systems is certainly a reflection of this unfortunate inclination.

ColourSpectrums provides the best of both worlds: a quick and efficient way of understanding the four basic functions that everyone uses while not categorizing or labelling people. In fact, ColourSpectrums respects everyone's individuality and celebrates each person's unique use of these four colour functions.

ColourSpectrums is Different

You may be familiar with personality typing models that create personality categories and then create questionnaires that are designed to force you into one of those pre-determined categories, temperaments or types. ColourSpectrums is different. ColourSpectrums defines four dimensions of human development that every person has. Rather than categorizing the person, I categorize the behaviours and characteristics. The applications are reversed. It is not, "There are four kinds of people." It is, "Every person has four functions."

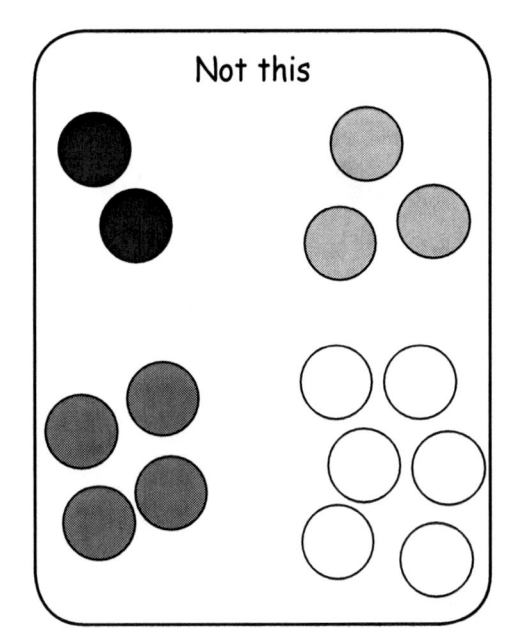

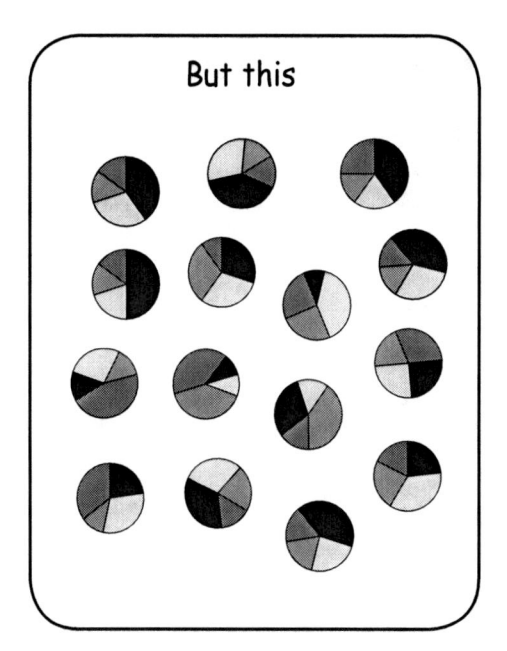

Section 2: ColourSpectrums Implications for You and Others

Personality typing systems are stereotyping systems that assume everyone in the same category has the same characteristics and behaviours. This is not helpful. More importantly, this is not true. In ColourSpectrums if you are behaving in a certain way you can determine what colour you are using. We couldn't say all people with bright red play soccer, but we could say all people playing soccer are using bright red. Rather than fitting people into a limited number of categories, there are an infinite number of ColourSpectrums and each individual person has a unique one.

Using the ColourSpectrums Language

While it is not helpful to label yourself as a colour, it <u>is</u> useful to use the ColourSpectrums language to refer to the "blue" part of yourself, the "green" part of yourself, the "red" part of yourself, and the "yellow" part of yourself.

For example:
"My blue is feeling disappointed."
"My green is confused."
"My red is pumped up and eager to go!"
"I haven't been using my yellow organization lately."

It is also effective to use the ColourSpectrums language to refer to other people's "blue," "green," "red," and "yellow."

For example:
"I sense you are genuinely in touch with your blue emotions."
"How is your green understanding this?"
"I see your red has really kicked in!"
"This yellow scheduling seems really important to you."

Rob Chubb

Card Descriptions in Detail

The following exercise will lead you to a deeper understanding and appreciation of the complex functions of your four colours. Refer to the ColourSpectrums card descriptions during the following activities.

Read the descriptions on the blue ColourSpectrums card.

Read the blue "I" statements one at a time and visualize the blue part of yourself as being the "I" in each statement.

For example:

> **I AM PERSONAL: I FACILITATE HARMONIOUS RELATIONSHIPS.**
> I am friendly and enjoy warm-hearted interactions.
> I relate genuinely and attach emotionally.

Your blue will identify more closely with some statements than with others. If blue is one of your brighter colours you will identify closely with many of them but not all to the same extent. If your blue is pale you will not identify closely with many of the statements but you will identify more closely with some of them. In other words, regardless of how bright or pale your blue is in your ColourSpectrums personality there will be variations in intensity within your blue spectrum. The same is true of your other colours.

Read the descriptions on the green ColourSpectrums card.

Read the green "I" statements one at a time and visualize the green part of yourself as being the "I" in each statement.

For example:

> **I AM ANALYTICAL: I CONCEPTUALIZE NEW IDEAS.**
> I have a curious mind and want to know more.
> I am theoretical, intrigued by mysteries and possibilities.

Your green will identify more closely with some statements than with others. If your green is bright, not all statements will be equally bright. If your green is pale not all statements will be equally pale.

Section 2: ColourSpectrums Implications for You and Others

Read the descriptions on the red ColourSpectrums card.

Read the red "I" statements one at a time and visualize the red part of yourself as being the "I" in each statement.

For example:

> **I AM PHYSICAL: I TAKE IMMEDIATE ACTION.**
> I am physically active, living moment to moment.
> I act immediately on impulse to maximize opportunities.

How did your red respond to each statement? Your red will identify more closely with some statements than with others.

Read the descriptions on the yellow ColourSpectrums card.

Read each of the yellow "I" statements one at a time and visualize the yellow part of yourself as being the "I" in each statement.

For example:

> **I AM ORGANIZED: I ESTABLISH AND MAINTAIN ORDER.**
> I am dedicated, reliable and prepared to serve.
> I am trustworthy and diligent in my duties.

Your yellow will identify more closely with some statements than with others

Each of your colours has a variety of shades and a range of diverse intensities. As bright as your brightest colour is, it is unlikely that every description on that card is equally bright for you. This also means that other people who have the same brightest colour as you do not use all the characteristics with the same intensity as you. As pale as your palest colour is, it is unlikely that every descriptions on that card is equally pale for you, which also means that people who have the same palest colour as you do not use all those characteristics with the same pale intensity that you do.

Consider your middle colours as well. You will identify more closely with some of those statements and less closely with others. People who have the same middle colours as you will also use those colours in different ways and with different intensities.

Five Distinct and Separate Senses

We have five senses. We have the senses of seeing, hearing, touching, smelling and tasting. Each of your five sensory organs processes different sensory information and performs distinctly separate and unique functions that are not replicated by the other sensory organs. Your eyes, for example, perceive and process light. This visual information gives you the sense of sight but your eyes cannot hear, touch, smell or taste anything. Your ears perceive and process sound waves — auditory information to give you the sense of hearing — but your ears cannot see (not even a little bit), touch, smell or taste anything. Your skin perceives pressure and temperature. This tactile information gives you the sense of touch, but your skin cannot see, hear, smell or taste anything. Your nose processes odours to give the sense of smell, but your nose cannot see, hear, touch or taste anything. Your taste buds process flavours to give you the sense of taste, but your taste buds cannot see, hear, touch or smell anything. Each of your five senses performs a distinct and separate function. The key point is that there are no duplication of services.

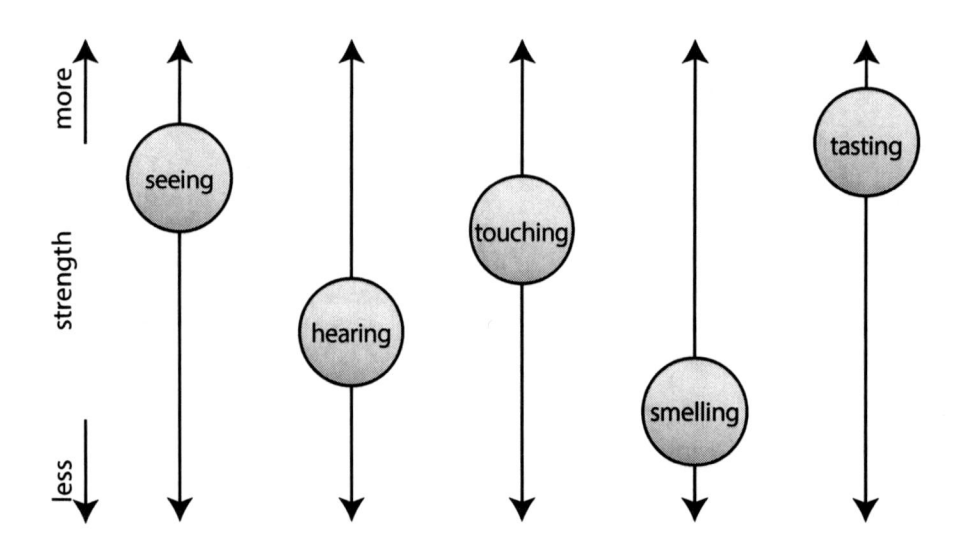

> Your five senses function simultaneously with no duplication of services.

The 5 senses function simultaneously along distinct and separate continuums of strength with no duplication of services.

You can see in the illustration that an increase or decrease in the functioning of one of the senses does not change the functioning or sensitivity of the other senses. Close your eyes and you can still hear. Plug your ears and you can still smell, and so on.

Our five senses function in a synchronized manner to provide a fully integrated sensory experience in which we see, hear, touch, smell and taste simultaneously. Imagine a friend calling your name and tossing a ripe red apple to you. You catch

Section 2: ColourSpectrums Implications for You and Others

it, take it in hand, take a bite and smell the fruity aroma and taste the scrumptious sweet flavour. Without being consciously aware of it, your five senses have worked flawlessly together in a coordinated way to process the five sensory dimensions of this experience. Your ears hear your friend call your name, your eyes see the red apple flying through the air toward you, your sensory body memory remembers that catching an apple is different than catching a basketball, your hand-eye coordination enables you to catch the apple, raise it to your mouth and sink your teeth into it with just the right amount of pressure to bite off a crisp mouth-watering, bite-size chunk. Your sense of smell and sense of taste combine to reveal the delicious flavour that bursts from the luscious fresh ripe red apple.

Four Distinct and Separate Colours

As separate as our five sensory functions are, we do not experience these sensory events as fragmented or disjointed; incredibly, we experience these simultaneous multisensory events as seamless, integrated, holistic experiences.

Think about how your five senses function. That is how your four colours function!

This is how your five senses function: separate functions operating simultaneously without duplication of services. This is also how your four colours function: separate functions operating simultaneously without duplication of services. The fact that there are no duplication of functions makes this system highly efficient.

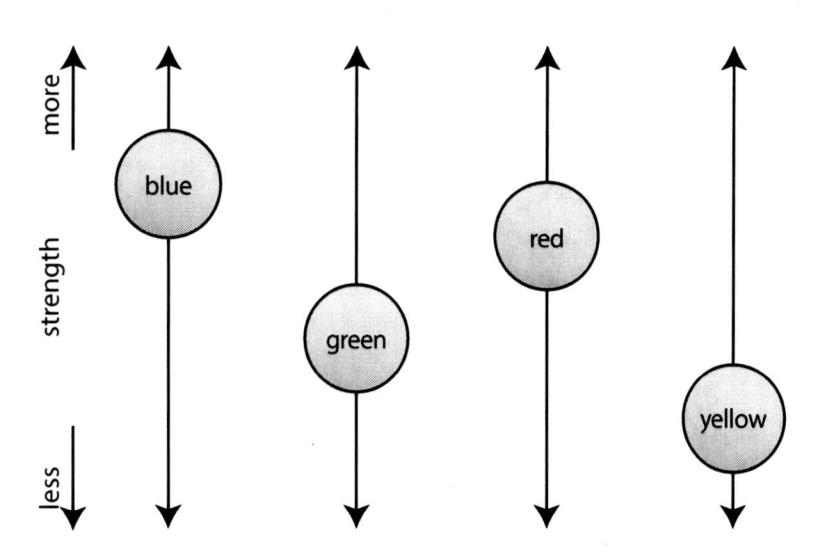

The 4 colours function simultaneously along distinct and separate continuums of strength with no duplication of services.

Each of your four colours performs unique and separate functions that are not replicated by the other three colours. Your blue performs emotional and spiritual functions and cannot perform green cognitive functions, red physical functions or yellow organizational functions. Your blue emotions are not logical or reasonable, they do not take physical action nor are they orderly, organized or predictable. Your green performs cognitive functions and cannot perform blue emotional functions, red physical functions or yellow organizational functions. Your green logic is not emotional, does not take physical action and is not organized or orderly. Your red is a real natural for performing physical functions but cannot perform blue emotional functions, green cognitive functions or yellow organizational functions. Your red physical body is not emotional, logical or orderly. Your yellow performs organizational functions and cannot perform blue emotional functions, green cognitive functions or red physical functions. Your yellow is not emotional or logical and it doesn't take action. While each colour performs exclusive functions that are not performed by other colours, they do function simultaneously.

As separate as our four colours' functions are, we do not experience them as fragmented or disjointed; incredibly we experience all four colours simultaneously as a seamless, integrated, holistic event. This is the human experience.

The blue pendulum of emotions swings back and forth along a continuum of emotional states, between intense blue emotions at the bright end and diminished emotions at the pale end. These "mood swings" or moods swing between feeling more emotional and feeling less emotional, between feeling attached and feeling unattached, between feeling more spiritual and feeling less spiritual.

The green pendulum of thought swings back and forth along a continuum of cognitive states, between intense green thinking at the bright end and minimal green thinking at the other end, between making sense and not making sense, between being rational and irrational, between being logical and illogical, and between thinking more and thinking less.

The red pendulum of physical activity alternates between physical actions at the bright end of the continuum and inactions at the pale end of the continuum, between doing and not doing, between being physically active and being physically inactive, between being awake and being asleep.

The yellow pendulum of order swings back and forth along a continuum of organizational states, between order and chaos, between organization and disorganization, between being prepared and being unprepared, between being on track and being off track or losing track, and between being in control and being out of control.

Think of the colours in the illustration as sliders that you can move up and down to increase and decrease the strengths of each function the same way you can move the slide controls on a sound system equalizer. Changing the strength of one range of frequencies does not change any of the other frequencies, but it does have a dramatic effect on the overall sound.

> "The pendulum of the mind alternates between sense and nonsense, not between right and wrong."
>
> — Carl Jung

In the same way, increasing or decreasing the strengths of one colour does not change the strengths of any other colours, but it does have a dramatic effect on the over all effect. Your particular combination of colour strengths is your colour spectrum. It is this overall effect that people know as your "personality."

Section 2: ColourSpectrums Implications for You and Others

While these four colours perform distinct and separate functions, when we use them together in a coordinated manner we are fully functioning and highly effective, living life to the fullest.

Your five senses do not have opposites. Seeing, for example, is not the opposite of hearing. Touching is not the opposite of tasting and so on. Your five senses are clearly different but not opposites. Your four colours do not have opposites either. Your colours perform clearly different functions but they are not opposites. Blue emotions are not the opposite of green thoughts, for example, and red actions are not the opposite of yellow orderliness. Your colours perform different, not opposite, functions.

Four Distinct and Separate Developmental Functions

ColourSpectrums is a developmental model. Each colour represents a specific dimension of human growth that is continually developing along its own distinct and separate developmental continuum.

Refer to the four card descriptions. Let's take a look at each of these card descriptions again, this time from four different perspectives.

Exclusive blue functions

1) Take a moment to get in touch with the blue part of your self, your blue emotional and spiritual energy.

2) Now, read some of the green, red and yellow card descriptions as if your blue is reading them, as if your blue is the "I" in each of those statements.

What happened? As it turns out your blue cannot identify with green, red, or yellow statements because your blue does not perform those functions.

This exercise and the following similar exercises are like trying to use your eyes to hear, touch, smell or taste something. Or like using your ears to see, touch, smell or taste something. It just doesn't work because your eyes do not perform functions other than seeing and your ears do not perform functions other than hearing and so on.

Your blue only performs the functions on the blue card. Your blue can feel but it cannot think, act, or organize.

Exclusive green functions

1) Take a moment to think about the green part of yourself, your green mental energy.

2) Now, read some of the blue, red and yellow card descriptions as if your green is reading them, as if your green is the "I" in each of those statements.

What happened? Just as before, your green cannot identify with blue, red or yellow statements because your green only performs the functions on the green card. Your green can think but it cannot feel, act, or organize.

When people experience deep blue emotions you may hear them say, "Words cannot express how I feel" or "I am at a loss for words." This is because the intellectual process of thinking of words to explain and articulate blue emotions is actually an attempt to use the green cognitive function to interpret and express a blue experience; it does not work. Words are a green cognitive language, and emotions are a blue emotional experience. The reason that it seems so difficult to put feelings into words is that it is more than difficult, it is impossible, impossible to use green words to adequately express blue emotions. Your green can interpret, explain and articulate, but it cannot experience or adequately convey blue emotions. Green cannot perform blue functions. Neither can blue perform green functions. Words can never fully convey how emotions are experienced... only true blue empathy comes close because empathy warms the soul. Your green cannot empathize, even though it thinks it can. It cannot empathize with some one else's blue emotions. The implications for you are important. Your green logical thoughts cannot empathize with your blue emotions.

Exclusive red functions

1) Take a moment to get a sense of your red physical body, your red physical energy. Red includes your five senses.

2) Now, read some of the blue, green and yellow card descriptions as if your red is reading them, as if your red is the "I" in each of those statements.

What happened? Your red physical body cannot identify with blue, green, or yellow statements because your red does not perform those functions. Your red only performs the functions on the red card. Your red can physically act but it cannot feel, think, or organize.

Exclusive yellow functions

1) Take a moment to focus on the yellow part of your self, your yellow organizational energy.

2) Now, read some of the blue, green and red card descriptions as if your yellow is reading them, as if your yellow is the "I" in each of those statements.

What happened? Your yellow cannot identify with blue, green, or red statements because your yellow does not perform those functions. Your yellow only performs the functions on the yellow card. Your yellow can organize and maintain order but it cannot feel, think, or act.

Section 2: ColourSpectrums Implications for You and Others

Proverbs

There are four proverbs on each of the four ColourSpectrums attribute cards. A proverb is a traditional saying which offers advice or presents a moral in a short and pithy manner. The wisdom of proverbs crosses cultural boundaries; they reveal universal human values. As you review the following proverbs you will not only recognize many of them but you will also realize that many proverbs espouse the merits of one colour or another.

Blue Proverbs

The following blue proverbs are listed on the blue attribute card.

> *"Faith moves mountains."*
> *"Love makes the world go around."*
> *"Do unto others as you would have them do unto you."*
> *"To understand people, you must walk a mile in their shoes."*

More blue proverbs

A friend in need is a friend in deed.

A soft answer turneth away wrath.

Absence makes the heart grow fonder.

Beauty is in the eye of the beholder.

Honey catches more flies than vinegar.

Hope springs eternal.

It is better to give than to receive.

Know thyself.

Love conquers all.

Love will find a way.

One good turn deserves another.

The eyes are the windows to the soul.

The road to a friend is never long.

The more the merrier.

To err is human, to forgive is divine.

Rob Chubb

Green Proverbs

The following green proverbs are listed on the green attribute card.

> *"Knowledge is power."*
> *"Wonders never cease."*
> *"I think; therefore, I am."*
> *"It is never too late to learn."*

More green proverbs

A word to the wise is sufficient.

First think, then speak.

Garbage in, garbage out.

Great minds think alike.

He that knows nothing, doubts nothing.

Necessity is the mother of invention.

Out of the mouths of babes.

The more one knows, the less one believes.

There are two sides to every question.

There is no such thing as a dumb question.

Things are not always what they seem.

Think first and think afterwards.

Truth will out.

Two heads are better than one.

Who knows most, speaks last.

Red Proverbs

The following red proverbs are listed on the red attribute card.

> *"Variety is the spice of life."*
> *"Make hay while the sun shines."*
> *"Actions speak louder than words."*
> *"Nothing ventured, nothing gained."*

More red proverbs

A change is as good as a rest.

A rolling stone gathers no moss.

All the world is a stage.

Easy come, easy go.

Section 2: ColourSpectrums Implications for You and Others

If you are not living on the edge, you are taking up too much space.

Laughter is the best medicine.

No pain, no gain.

No time like the present.

She who hesitates is lost.

The early bird catches the worm.

Tomorrow never comes.

We are here for a good time, not long time.

What you see is what you get.

When all else fails... read the directions.

Where there's a will, there's a way.

Yellow Proverbs

The following yellow proverbs are listed on the yellow attribute card.

> *"Waste not, want not."*
> *"Better safe than sorry."*
> *"A penny saved is a penny earned."*
> *"A place for everything and everything in its place."*

More yellow proverbs

An ounce of prevention is worth a pound of cure.

Business before pleasure.

Cleanliness is next to Godliness.

Diligence is the mother of good fortune.

Don't put all your eggs in one basket.

Don't put the cart before the horse.

Dot your i's and cross your t's.

First things first.

Haste makes waste.

If a job is worth doing, it's worth doing well.

If it ain't broke, don't fix it.

If you fail to plan, you plan to fail.

Measure twice, cut once.

Mind your p's and q's.

Take it one step at a time.

Speaking of proverbs there is one that says that one step leads to the next. So what is the next step?

Endings and Beginnings

This book is an introduction to ColourSpectrums. I am confident that the fundamental principles and discoveries presented here will contribute significantly to your personal and professional development. These foundations set the stage for the next step in this exciting ColourSpectrums journey of discovery. In the next book, ColourSpectrums 2: Stress Management and Conflict Resolution, you will learn how to maximize self-esteem and reduce stress. You will learn about bright and pale shadows. You will learn how to be a great communicator. In the third book, ColourSpectrums 3: Brightening Pale Colours, you will learn how to empower all of your colours and use them in a balanced and highly effective manner.

ColourSpectrums Applications

The journey and discoveries continue. ColourSpectrums continues to develop with a view to advancing personal and professional effectiveness and human understanding. I encourage you to visit our website www.colourspectrums.com for current developments, new applications and learning opportunities.

ColourSpectrums workshops have been presented to diverse groups around the world.

Diverse applications of ColourSpectrums include:

- Anti-bullying
- Business Management
- Career Counselling
- Career Development
- Child Care
- Child Development
- Communication Skills
- Community Relations
- Conflict Resolution
- Correctional Services
- Couples Communication
- Customer Service
- Family Communication
- Family Dynamics
- Family Violence Prevention
- Foster Parenting
- Learning Styles
- Life Skills
- Marketing
- Marriage Preparation
- Parenting Styles
- Personal Counseling
- Rehabilitation Services
- Self-Esteem
- Solution Focus
- Stress Management
- Supervision
- Teaching Styles
- Team Building
- Team Diversity
- Team Esteem
- Youth Development
- Youth at Risk
- Values Clarification

About the Author

Rob Chubb was born in Grande Prairie, Alberta, in 1951. Rob is the middle child of five children. His father was a United Church minister and his mother, a former nurse, dedicated herself to raising the family of four boys and one girl. Rob lived in Alberta and British Columbia until the age of 15 when he moved with his family to California. He graduated from North Hollywood High School in 1969. When he returned to Canada he worked extensively with children and youth at risk throughout western Canada. In 1976 he graduated from Grant MacEwan College in Edmonton with a diploma in Child and Youth Care. He was a faculty member at MacEwan for the next 20 years. He also graduated with his girlfriend Laurie. They married in 1978 and live in Sherwood Park, Alberta. They have five adult children. In 1997 Rob graduated from the University of Victoria, B.C., with a Bachelor's Degree (with distinction) in Child and Youth Care. Rob and Laurie have been foster parents to over 20 children during the last 25 years. They have managed group homes for at-risk pregnant teens, managed a group home in Cambridge Bay in the Arctic and dedicated their lives to improving the lives of children and families. Rob has worked extensively as a foster parent trainer for the Government of Alberta and in Australia.

Rob is the author and director of ColourSpectrums promoting human development and self-empowerment through education, interaction and fun. Rob presents regularly at local, provincial, national and international venues. He has presented ColourSpectrums to over 20,000 participants over the past 15 years. Clients include Government, Educational, Business, non-profit and private agencies. Rob has trained over 1,000 facilitators throughout Canada, the United States and Australia.

Call for Facilitators

We are actively seeking people who would like to be trained and certified to present ColourSpectrums. ColourSpectrums is presented to groups only by certified facilitators. If you would like to be trained to present ColourSpectrums to groups or would like to participate in an in-depth session, please contact Rob at www.colourspectrums.com

Rob welcomes your enquiries and comments. You can contact him through www.colourspectrums.com

ColourSpectrums Personality Styles Book 1: The Introduction

Sort the cards to reveal your personality as a unique spectrum of:

Blue   Emotional intelligence
Green   Intellectual intelligence
Red   Physical intelligence
Yellow   Organizational intelligence

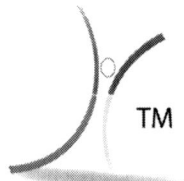

You are more intelligent than you "think"!

You will:
- Use four intelligences to make more intelligent choices
- Identify your bright colour strengths
- Acknowledge your pale colour challenges
- Easily identify anyone's ColourSpectrums personality
- Communicate more effectively and enhance relationships

Includes:
- Four Introductory Cards and scoring system
- Written exercises with individual and paired activities

Benefits:
- Personal, professional and team development for:
Leaders, managers, students, coaches, educators and families
Thousands have benefitted. You can too!

This ground-breaking work synthesizes personality styles into one seamless developmental model.

"So brilliantly simple, it's simply brilliant!"
"Profoundly insightful aha! learning."
"Entertaining ha-ha! learning."
"Hands-on practical and user friendly."

In the series:

ColourSpectrums Personality Styles Book 1: The Introduction
ColourSpectrums Personality Styles Book 2: Stress Management and Conflict Resolution
ColourSpectrums Personality Styles Book 3: Brightening Pale Colours

Author

Rob Chubb is the founding director and author of ColourSpectrums. Rob has trained over 1,000 ColourSpectrums facilitators worldwide. He draws from a wealth of practical experience and dynamic presentations to diverse audiences of children, youth and adults including local agencies, national organizations and multinational corporations. Rob is the father of five children and lives with his wife, Laurie, in Sherwood Park, Alberta.

www.colourspectrums.com

ColourSpectrums Personality Styles Book 2: Stress Management and Conflict Resolution

Sort the Stress Management Cards to reveal your:

Blue   Shadow characteristics
Green   Shadow characteristics
Red   Shadow characteristics
Yellow   Shadow characteristics

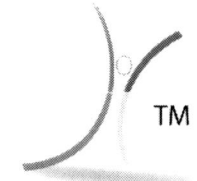

*Bright colours are how you are.
Pale colours are how you are not
(which is how you are...not).*

You will:
- Identify bright colour needs, stressors and shadow behaviours
- Acknowledge pale colour challenges, stressors and shadow behaviours
- Understand fight and flight dynamics
- Easily identify anyone's shadow characteristics
- Brighten and diminish your colours to reduce stress and conflict

Includes:
- Four Stress Management/Conflict Resolution Cards
- Written exercises with individual and paired activities

Benefits:
- Personal, professional and team development for:
  Leaders, managers, students, coaches, educators and families
  Thousands have benefitted. You can too!

This ground-breaking work synthesizes personality styles into one seamless developmental model.

"So brilliantly simple, it's simply brilliant!"
"Profoundly insightful aha! learning."
"Entertaining ha-ha! learning."
"Hands-on practical and user friendly."

In the series:

ColourSpectrums Personality Styles Book 1: The Introduction
ColourSpectrums Personality Styles Book 2: Stress Management and Conflict Resolution
ColourSpectrums Personality Styles Book 3: Brightening Pale Colours

Author

Rob Chubb is the founding director and author of ColourSpectrums. Rob has trained over 1,000 ColourSpectrums facilitators worldwide. He draws from a wealth of practical experience and dynamic presentations to diverse audiences of children, youth and adults including local agencies, national organizations and multinational corporations. Rob is the father of five children and lives with his wife, Laurie, in Sherwood Park, Alberta.

www.colourspectrums.com

ColourSpectrums Personality Styles Book 3: Brightening Pale Colours

Use Brightening Cards and In-ChargeCards to brighten pale colours:

Blue   Emotional skills
Green Cognitive skills
Red   Physical skills
Yellow Organizational skills

TM

*Who you are is constant.
How you are is
constantly changing.*

You will:
- Learn the common phrases, voice tone and pace of each colour
- Recognize each colour's body language
- Brighten your palest colour
- Use four colours to communicate effectively
- Use four colour to balance your life

Includes:
- Four Brightening Cards with goal setting In-ChargeCards
- Written exercises with individual and paired activities

Benefits:
- Personal, professional and team development for:
Leaders, managers, students, coaches, educators and families
Thousands have benefitted. You can too!

This ground-breaking work synthesizes personality styles into one seamless developmental model.

"So brilliantly simple, it's simply brilliant!"
"Profoundly insightful aha! learning."
"Entertaining ha-ha! learning."
"Hands-on practical and user friendly."

In the series:

ColourSpectrums Personality Styles Book 1: The Introduction
ColourSpectrums Personality Styles Book 2: Stress Management and Conflict Resolution
ColourSpectrums Personality Styles Book 3: Brightening Pale Colours

Author

Rob Chubb is the founding director and author of ColourSpectrums. Rob has trained over 1,000 ColourSpectrums facilitators worldwide. He draws from a wealth of practical experience and dynamic presentations to diverse audiences of children, youth and adults including local agencies, national organizations and multinational corporations. Rob is the father of five children and lives with his wife, Laurie, in Sherwood Park, Alberta.

www.colourspectrums.com

Enjoy all three books in this series:

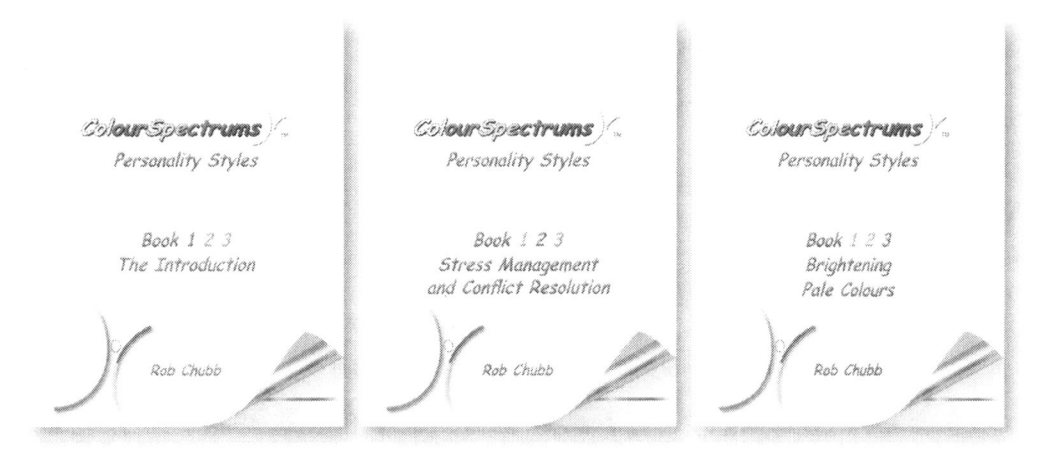

1) Order by phone 780-922-6877
2) Order on line at www.colourspectrums.com
3) Fax (780-922-6877) or Mail this form to: ColourSpectrums
   #13, 53046 Range Road 222
   Ardrossan, Alberta   T8E 2E8
   Canada

Your name _____

Address _____

_____

City _____

Province/State _____   Postal Code _____

Quantity	Stock #	Product Description	Unit Price	Total
	CS 022	ColourSpectrums Personality Styles Book 1 The Introduction	$30.00 (includes $5.00 S&H)	
	CS 023	ColourSpectrums Personality Styles Book 2 Stress Management and Conflict Resolution	$30.00 (includes $5.00 S&H)	
	CS 024	ColourSpectrums Personality Styles Book 3 Brightening Pale Colours	$30.00 (includes $5.00 S&H)	
		Our GST #: 104085691	Subtotal	
			Add 5% GST	
			Total Payable	

Method of Payment: ☐ Visa   ☐ Mastercard

Card Number _____   Expiry Date _____

Card Holder's Name _____

Signature _____

Rob Chubb

Card Set

Blue

Blue

I AM PERSONAL: I FACILITATE HARMONIOUS RELATIONSHIPS.
I am friendly and enjoy warm-hearted interactions.
I relate genuinely and attach emotionally.

I am a gentle, kind and nurturing helper.
I empathize, comfort and convey emotional support.
I inspire people to be the best they can be.
I set aside my needs in order to accommodate others.

I feel deeply, expressing heart-felt emotions.
I am esteemed when appreciated for who I truly am.

I am humanistic: people come first.
I value harmonious interpersonal relationships.
I facilitate group consensus and foster group cohesion and rapport.

I am artistic and creative with a vivid imagination.
I am passionate about my work and give it a personal touch.
I feel valued as a person when my work is appreciated.
I ponder the meaning of life, believing everything has a purpose.

"Faith moves mountains."
"Love makes the world go around."
"Do unto others as you would have them do unto you."
"To understand people, you must walk a mile in their shoes."

I am relationship oriented:
PERSONABLE   KIND HEARTED   FRIENDLY

I focus on interpersonal interactions:
FRIENDSHIPS   RELATIONSHIPS   FELLOWSHIPS

I promote compassion, well-being, balance, peace and harmony:
HOLISTIC   BENEVOLENT   CONSIDERATE

I value personal growth and human development:
SELF-AWARENESS   SELF-EXPRESSION   SELF-ESTEEM

I am motivated by deep passions, **so I act** with feelings:
LOVE   SORROW   EMOTIONS

I am a naturally gifted caregiver, embracing human potential:
EMPATHIC   EMPOWERING   CONSOLING

I thrive in environments that are humanistic:
INTERPERSONAL   COOPERATIVE   AFFIRMING

I take pride in being genuine and sincere:
AFFECTIONATE   INTIMATE   CARING

In life I seek identity, authenticity, and purpose of being:
SPIRITUAL   SOUL-SEARCHING   FAITHFUL

ColourSpectrums Blue Attributes copyright 2001 Rob Chubb www.colourspectrums.com

Card Set

Green

Green

I AM ANALYTICAL: I CONCEPTUALIZE NEW IDEAS.
I have a curious mind and want to know more.
I am theoretical, intrigued by mysteries and possibilities.

I investigate thoroughly to fully comprehend.
I use precise wording to ensure I explain my ideas clearly.

I need to know why.
I observe, study and analyze to detect strategic information.
I use logic to evaluate ideas and improve them.
I formulate new theories, concepts and hypotheses.

I am matter-of-fact and say what's on my mind.
I think of unique solutions, improved strategies and innovations.
I suspect there is always more to something than is first apparent.
I perceive complexities in the simple and simplicities in the complex.

I value freedom of thought to understand truth and reality.
I encourage debate, new perspectives and futuristic thinking.
I need time alone to independently think things through.

"Knowledge is power."
"Wonders never cease."
"I think; therefore, I am."
"It is never too late to learn."

I am thought oriented:
REASONING   EXPLAINING   RATIONAL

I focus on theories and concepts:
CONTEMPLATING   SCRUTINIZING   PROBING

I promote unique perspectives and ingenious solutions:
VISIONARY   INNOVATIVE   INSIGHTFUL

I value information, data and logic:
FACTUAL   OBJECTIVE   SCIENTIFIC

I am motivated by curiousity, **so I act** with skepticism:
INQUISITIVE   PENSIVE   EXPLORING

I am a naturally gifted detective asking thought provoking questions:
INVESTIGATING   RESEARCHING   EXAMINING

I thrive in environments where I can explore and ponder possibilities:
OBSERVING   SPECULATING   DISCOVERING

I take pride in having a mind of my own:
SELF-DETERMINED   SELF-RELIANT   AUTONOMOUS

In life I seek intellectual competence:
DELIBERATING   FORMULATING   SOLVING

ColourSpectrums Green Attributes copyright 2001 Rob Chubb www.colourspectrums.com

Card Set

Red

Red

I AM PHYSICAL: I TAKE IMMEDIATE ACTION.
I am physically active, living moment to moment.
I act immediately on impulse to maximize opportunities.

I feel lucky.
I test my nerve and skills by taking risks.
I pursue tangible "hands-on" activities.
I eagerly handle tools, operate equipment and run machines.
I seek firsthand experiences and exciting adventures.

I enjoy the thrill of competition and excel under pressure.
I perform skillfully when I have room to move.
I acquire a repertoire of high-performance skills and talents.

I am lively, entertaining and on the go.
I initiate action with a can-do attitude.
I promote playfulness, humour and active participation.

I live it up in the fast lane and thrive on good times.
I am full of life, living life to the fullest.

"Variety is the spice of life."
"Make hay while the sun shines."
"Actions speak louder than words."
"Nothing ventured, nothing gained."

I am action oriented:
| DYNAMIC | UP AND ABOUT | ON THE GO |

I focus on here-and-now opportunities:
| IMMEDIATELY | PROACTIVELY | IN THE MOMENT |

I promote action with my positive, upbeat, optimistic attitude:
| ENTHUSIASTIC | PLAYFUL | RESILIENT |

I value living on the edge:
| THRILL SEEKING | RISK TAKING | FUN LOVING |

I am motivated by sudden urges, **so I act** impulsively:
| INSTANTANEOUSLY | SPONTANEOUSLY | QUICKLY |

I am a naturally gifted adventurer:
| SENSATION SEEKER | SELF-STARTER | GO-GETTER |

I thrive in environments where I move freely:
| PERFORMING | MULTITASKING | STIMULATING |

I take pride in the impact of my energetic actions and skills:
| GIVE IT A WHIRL | IMPROVISE | WING IT |

In life I seek diverse, hands-on experiences and adventures:
| CHALLENGING | EXCITING | DARING |

ColourSpectrums Red Attributes copyright 2001 Rob Chubb www.colourspectrums.com

Card Set

Yellow

87

Yellow

I AM ORGANIZED: I ESTABLISH AND MAINTAIN ORDER.
I am dedicated, reliable and prepared to serve.
I am trustworthy and diligent in my duties.

I want plans decided and tasks assigned.
I use checklists, timetables, calendars and schedules.
I prioritize tasks and do them in order.
I value the responsibility of being in charge and accountable.

I judge right from wrong and comply with authority.
I am a stabilizer, adhering to standard operating procedures.

I value membership in established organizations and institutions.
I work consistently to be a conscientious, solid citizen.
I follow customs and routines which give me a sense of security.
I like familiar settings where things are arranged safely and soundly.

I like task-oriented, businesslike transactions.
I save, invest, safeguard, budget and spend money economically.
I take responsibilities, commitments and obligations seriously.

"Waste not, want not."
"Better safe than sorry."
"A penny saved is a penny earned."
"A place for everything and everything in its place."

I am role oriented:
| RELIABLE | HARD WORKING | ACCOUNTABLE |

I focus on tasks because work comes first:
| PLANNING | PREPARING | ORGANIZING |

I promote standards and respect for authority:
| CONFORMITY | LAW AND ORDER | DISCIPLINE |

I value roles and responsibilities:
| BEING IN CHARGE | BEING OF SERVICE | BEING A MEMBER |

I am motivated by a strong sense of duty, **so I act** responsibly:
| PRIORITIES | COMMITMENTS | FOLLOW-THROUGH |

I am a naturally gifted organizer people can depend on:
| SYSTEMATIC | SEQUENTIAL | DETAILED |

I thrive in environments that are predictable:
| ROUTINES | TRADITIONS | INSTITUTIONS |

I take pride in my dependability and a job properly done:
| ON TASK | ON TIME | ON SCHEDULE |

In life I seek responsibilities and earned social status:
| TRUSTWORTHY | STEADFAST | ESTABLISHED |

ColourSpectrums Yellow Attributes copyright 2001 Rob Chubb www.colourspectrums.com